THE **W**ORD ON

THE OLD TESTAMENT

KARA ECKMANN

JIM BURNS, GENERAL EDITOR

THE NATIONAL INSTITUTE OF YOUTH MINISTRY

Gospel Light

Gospel Light is an evangelical Christian publisher dedicated to serving the local church. We believe God's vision for Gospel Light is to provide church leaders with biblical, user-friendly materials that will help them evangelize, disciple and minister to children, youth and families.

We hope this Gospel Light resource will help you discover biblical truth for your own life and help you minister to youth. God bless you in your work.

For a free catalog of resources from Gospel Light please contact your Christian supplier or call 1-800-4-GOSPEL.

PUBLISHING STAFF
William T. Greig, Publisher
Dr. Elmer L. Towns, Senior Consulting Publisher
Dr. Gary S. Greig, Senior Consulting Editor
Jean Daly, Managing Editor
Pam Weston, Editorial Assistant
Kyle Duncan, Associate Publisher
Bayard Taylor, M.Div., Editor, Theological and Biblical Issues
Cathy Burns, Contributing Writer
Debi Thayer, Designer

ISBN 0-8307-1726-9
© 1996 by Jim Burns

HOW TO MAKE CLEAN COPIES FROM THIS BOOK

YOU MAY MAKE COPIES OF PORTIONS OF THIS BOOK WITH A CLEAN CONSCIENCE IF:

- you (or someone in your organization) are the original purchaser;
- you are using the copies you make for a noncommercial purpose (such as teaching or promoting your ministry) within your church or organization;
- you follow the instructions provided in this book.

HOWEVER, IT IS **ILLEGAL** FOR YOU TO MAKE COPIES IF:

- you are using the material to promote, advertise or sell a product or service other than for ministry fund-raising;
- you are using the material in or on a product for sale;
- you or your organization are **not** the original purchaser of this book.

By following these guidelines you help us keep our products affordable.
Thank you,
Gospel Light

PRAISE FOR YOUTHBUILDERS

Jim Burns knows young people. He also knows how to communicate to them. This study should be in the hands of every youth leader interested in discipling young people.

David Adams, Vice President, Lexington Baptist College

I deeply respect and appreciate the groundwork Jim Burns has prepared for true teenage discernment. *YouthBuilders* is timeless in the sense that the framework has made it possible to plug into any society, at any point in time, and to proceed to discuss, experience and arrive at sincere moral and Christian conclusions that will lead to growth and life changes. Reaching young people may be more difficult today than ever before, but God's grace is alive and well in Jim Burns and this wonderful curriculum.

Fr. Angelo J. Artemas, Youth Ministry Director, Greek Orthodox Archdiocese of North and South America

I heartily recommend Jim Burns's *YouthBuilders Group Bible Studies* because they are leader-friendly tools that are ready to use in youth groups and Sunday School classes. Jim addresses the tough questions that students are genuinely facing every day and, through his engaging style, challenges young people to make their own decisions to move from their current opinions to God's convictions taught in the Bible. Every youth group will benefit from this excellent curriculum.

Paul Borthwick, Minister of Missions, Grace Chapel

Jim Burns recognizes the fact that small groups are where life change happens. In this study he has captured the essence of that value. Further, Jim has given much thought to shaping this very effective material into a usable tool that serves the parent, leader and student.

Bo Boshers, Executive Director, Student Impact, Willow Creek Community Church

It is about time that someone who knows kids, understands kids and works with kids writes youth curriculum that youth workers, both volunteer and professional, can use. Jim Burns's *YouthBuilders Group Bible Studies* is the curriculum that youth ministry has been waiting a long time for.

Ridge Burns, President,
The Center for Student Missions

Jim Burns has done it again. He speaks to kids right where they are and helps them to understand what Christianity is about in their own terms.

Tony Campolo, Professor, Eastern College

There are very few people in the world who know how to communicate life-changing truth effectively to teens. Jim Burns is one of the best. *YouthBuilders Group Bible Studies* puts handles on those skills and makes them available to everyone. These studies are biblically sound, hands-on practical and just plain fun. This one gets a five-star endorsement—which isn't bad since there are only four stars to start with.

Ken Davis, President, Dynamic Communications

I don't know anyone who knows and understands the needs of the youth worker like Jim Burns. His new curriculum not only reveals his knowledge of youth ministry but also his depth and sensitivity to the Scriptures. *YouthBuilders Group Bible Studies* is solid, easy to use and gets students out of their seats and into the Word. I've been waiting for something like this for a long time!

Doug Fields, Pastor of High School, Saddleback Valley Community Church

Jim Burns has a way of being creative without being "hokey." *YouthBuilders Group Bible Studies* takes the age-old model of curriculum and gives it a new look with tools such as the Bible *Tuck-In*™ and Parent Page. Give this new resource a try and you'll see that Jim shoots straightforward on tough issues. The *YouthBuilders* series is great for leading small-group discussions as well as teaching a large class of junior high or high school students. The Parent Page will help you get support from your parents in that they will understand the topics you are dealing with in your group. Put Jim's years of experience to work for you by equipping yourself with this quality material.

Curt Gibson, Pastor to Junior High, First Church of the Nazarene of Pasadena

Once again, Jim Burns has managed to handle very timely issues with just the right touch. His *YouthBuilders Group Bible Studies* succeeds in teaching solid biblical values without being stuffy or preachy. The format is user-friendly, designed to stimulate high involvement and deep discussion. Especially impressive is the Parent Page, a long overdue tool to help parents become part of the Christian education loop. I look forward to using it with my kids!

David M. Hughes, Pastor, First Baptist Church, Winston-Salem

What do you get when you combine a deep love for teens, over 20 years' experience in youth ministry and an excellent writer? You get Jim Burns's *YouthBuilders* series! This stuff has absolutely hit the nail on the head. Quality Sunday School and small-group material is tough to come by these days, but Jim has put every ounce of creativity he has into these books.

Greg Johnson, author of *Getting Ready for the Guy/Girl Thing* and *Keeping Your Cool While Sharing Your Faith*

Jim Burns has a gift, the gift of combining the relational and theological dynamics of our faith in a graceful, relevant and easy-to-chew-and-swallow way. *YouthBuilders Group Bible Studies* is a hit, not only for teens but for teachers.

Gregg Johnson, National Youth Director, International Church of the Foursquare Gospel

The practicing youth worker always needs more ammunition. Here is a whole book full of practical, usable resources for those facing kids face-to-face. *YouthBuilders Group Bible Studies* will get that blank stare off the faces of kids in your youth meeting!

Jay Kesler, President, Taylor University

I couldn't be more excited about the *YouthBuilders Group Bible Studies*. It couldn't have arrived at a more needed time. Spiritually we approach the future engaged in war with young people taking direct hits from the devil. This series will practically help teens who feel partially equipped to "put on the whole armor of God."

Mike MacIntosh, Pastor, Horizon Christian Fellowship

In *YouthBuilders Group Bible Studies*, Jim Burns pulls together the key ingredients for an effective curriculum series. Jim captures the combination of teen involvement and a solid biblical perspective, with topics that are relevant and straightforward. This series will be a valuable tool in the local church.

Dennis "Tiger" McLuen, Executive Director, Youth Leadership

My ministry takes me to the lost kids in our nation's cities where youth games and activities are often irrelevant and plain Bible knowledge for the sake of learning is unattractive. Young people need the information necessary to make wise decisions related to everyday problems. *YouthBuilders* will help many young people integrate their faith into everyday life, which after all is our goal as youth workers.

Miles McPherson, President, Project Intercept

Jim Burns's passion for teens, youth workers and parents of teens is evident in the *YouthBuilders Group Bible Studies*. He has a gift of presenting biblical truths on a level teens will fully understand, and youth workers and parents can easily communicate.

Al Menconi, President, Al Menconi Ministries

Youth ministry curriculum is often directed to only one spoke of the wheel of youth ministry—the adolescent. Not so with this material! Jim has enlarged the education circle, including information for the adolescent, the parent and the youth worker. *YouthBuilders Group Bible Studies* is youth and family ministry-oriented material at its best.

Helen Musick, Instructor of Youth Ministry, Asbury Seminary

Finally, a Bible study that has it all! It's action-packed, practical and biblical; but that's only the beginning. *YouthBuilders* involves students in the Scriptures. It's relational, interactive and leads

kids toward lifestyle changes. The unique aspect is a page for parents, something that's usually missing from adolescent curriculum. Jim Burns has outdone himself. This isn't a home run—it's a grand slam!

Dr. David Olshine, Director of Youth Ministries, Columbia International University

Here is a thoughtful and relevant curriculum designed to meet the needs of youth workers, parents and students. It's creative, interactive and biblical—and with Jim Burns's name on it, you know you're getting a quality resource.

Laurie Polich, Youth Director, First Presbyterian Church of Berkeley

In 10 years of youth ministry I've never used a curriculum because I've never found anything that actively involves students in the learning process, speaks to young people where they are and challenges them with biblical truth—I'll use this! *YouthBuilders Group Bible Studies* is a complete curriculum that is helpful to parents, youth leaders and, most importantly, today's youth.

Glenn Schroeder, Youth and Young Adult Ministries, Vineyard Christian Fellowship, Anaheim

This new material by Jim Burns represents a vitality in curriculum and, I believe, a more mature and faithful direction. *YouthBuilders Group Bible Studies* challenges youth by teaching them how to make decisions rather than telling them what decisions to make. Each session offers teaching concepts, presents options and asks for a decision. I believe it's healthy, the way Christ taught and represents the abilities, personhood and faithfulness of youth. I give it an *A+*!

J. David Stone, President, Stone & Associates

Jim Burns has done it again! This is a practical, timely and reality-based resource for equipping teens to live life in the fast-paced, pressure-packed adolescent world of the '90s. A very refreshing creative oasis in the curriculum desert!

Rich Van Pelt, President, Alongside Ministries

YouthBuilders Group Bible Studies is a tremendous new set of resources for reaching students. Jim has his finger on the pulse of youth today. He understands their mind-sets, and has prepared these studies in a way that will capture their attention and lead to greater maturity in Christ. I heartily recommend these studies.

Rick Warren, Senior Pastor,
Saddleback Valley Community Church

CONTENTS

THANKS AND
THANKS AGAIN!

A huge thanks to the following extraordinary people who have shaped me and thus this curriculum.

Thank you to Dolores, Michelle, Krista, Leslie and Annmarie for being phenomenal roommates up close and now e-mail soul mates from afar.

Thank you to Kim for sharpening me as iron sharpens iron first as my frosh Bible study leader and now as my friend.

Thank you to Chris for injecting life with a ton of laughter, movies, wisdom and fish tacos.

Thank you to Mike for seeing something in me that I couldn't see in myself and helping me catch a vision.

Thank you to the Lake Avenue students, staff and pastoral team for giving me a new home.

Thank you to my brothers and sisters—Matt, Laura, Laura and Jimie—for helping me laugh at myself and my love for peppermint ice cream.

Thank you to Dad and Helen for being a refuge from the storms of life.

Thank you to Mom and Jim for loving me with an unconditional and unbreakable love.

And, saving the best for last, thank you Jesus for being my Savior.

DEDICATION

To the person I respect the most in the whole world—my mom.

You taught me by your words and your example that when God calls, He always equips and provides. It is largely your prayers that strengthen and guide me. I count it an honor when people say I remind them of you!

Love,

Kara

YOUTHBUILDERS GROUP BIBLE STUDIES

It's Relational—Students learn best when they talk, not when you talk. There is always a get-acquainted section in the Warm Up. All the experiences are based on building community in your group.

It's Biblical—With no apologies, this series is unashamedly Christian. Every session has a practical, relevant Bible study.

It's Experiential—Studies show that young people retain up to 85 percent of the material when they are *involved* in action-oriented, experiential learning. The sessions use role-plays, discussion starters, case studies, graphs and other experiential, educational methods. *We believe it's a sin to bore a young person with the gospel.*

It's Interactive—This study is geared to get students feeling comfortable with sharing ideas and interacting with peers and leaders.

It's Easy to Follow—The sessions have been prepared by Jim Burns to allow the leader to pick up the material and use it. There is little preparation time on your part. Jim did the work for you.

It's Adaptable—You can pick and choose from several topics or go straight through the material as a whole study.

It's Age Appropriate—In the "Team Effort" section, one group experience relates best to junior high students while the other works better with high school students. Look at both to determine which option is best for your group.

It's Parent Oriented—The Parent Page helps you to do youth ministry at its finest. Christian education should take place in the home as well as in the church. The Parent Page is your chance to come alongside the parents and help them have a good discussion with their kids.

It's Proven—This material was not written by someone in an ivory tower. It was written for young people and has already been used with them. They love it.

HOW TO USE THIS STUDY

The 12 sessions are divided into three stand-alone units. Each unit has four sessions. You may choose to teach all 12 sessions consecutively. Or you may use only one unit. Or you may present individual sessions. You know your best so you choose.

Each of the 12 sessions is divided into five sections.

Warm Up—Young people will stay in your youth group if they feel comfortable and make friends in the group. This section is designed for you and the students to get to know each other better. These activities are filled with history-giving and affirming questions and experiences.

Team Effort—Following the model of Jesus, the Master Teacher, these activities engage young people in the session. Stories, group situations, surveys and more bring the session to the students. There is an option for junior high/middle school students and one for high school students.

In the Word—Most young people are biblically illiterate. These Bible studies present the Word of God and encourage students to see the relevance of the Scriptures to their lives.

Things to Think About—Young people need the opportunity to really think through the issues at hand. These discussion starters get students talking about the subject and interacting on important issues.

Parent Page—A youth worker can only do so much. Reproduce this page and get it into the hands of parents. This tool allows quality parent/teen communication that really brings the session home.

THE BIBLE *TUCK-IN*™

It's a tear-out sheet you fold and place in your Bible, containing the essentials you'll need for teaching your group.

HERE'S HOW TO USE IT:

To prepare for the session, first study the session. Tear out the Bible *Tuck-In*™ and personalize it by making notes. Fold the Bible *Tuck-In*™ in half on the dotted line. Slip it into your Bible for easy reference throughout the session. The Key Verse, Biblical Basis and Big Idea at the beginning of the Bible *Tuck-In*™ will help you keep the session on track. With the Bible *Tuck-In*™ your students will see that your teaching comes from the Bible and won't be distracted by a leader's guide.

EXTRAORDINARY BOOKS

LEADER'S PEP TALK

Imagine yourself walking into a party by yourself. You scan a sea of faces, searching for the four friends who said they would meet you there. Finally, you spot Dolores, Chris, Les and Annmarie standing in a circle in the far corner of the room near the food table. Weaving your way through the crowd, you arrive where your friends are standing. Dolores is in the middle of telling a story, but she stops as you greet your friends. Dolores resumes telling her story, which appears to be about two-thirds finished. When she concludes her story, your four friends burst out laughing, but you don't understand what's so funny. Why? You missed the first two-thirds of the story.

Let me ask you this question: How much of the story are you telling your students? There seems to be a nationwide youth ministry trend toward spending most of our time teaching students about the life of Christ, the writings of Paul and the stories of the Early Church; all of which are vital to Christian growth, but none of which capture the entire story of Scripture.

You may fear that your students will respond to your attempts to teach about the Old Testament with one word: "Boring." How far this is from the truth! The Old Testament is bursting with stories of conflict, war, envy, jealousy, miracles and healing. Anyone who views the Old Testament as boring has probably not read it—or maybe they spent all their time in Leviticus and Numbers!

This unit is designed to give your students an overview of four of the key books in the Old Testament. Each session is designed to give you a flavor of the overall book by analyzing one slice from it. Each session gives you the opportunity to interact with your students, helping them understand the life of the Old Testament.

Thank-you, dear friend, for being committed to helping students understand the complete story of Scripture. May you enjoy learning from its extraordinary adventures as well.

THE BOOK OF GENESIS:
CREATION AND CURSE

KEY VERSE

"'You will not surely die,' the serpent said to the woman. 'For God knows that when you eat of it your eyes will be opened, and you will be like God, knowing good and evil.'"
Genesis 3:4,5

BIBLICAL BASIS

Genesis 2:4—3:19;
Matthew 18:21-35;
1 Corinthians 1:25; 10:13;
2 Corinthians 12:9

THE BIG IDEA

We are God's creations, yet because of our sin we have been cursed.

AIMS OF THIS SESSION

During this session you will guide students to:
• Examine the fact that they are created by God;
• Discover the feelings of Adam, Eve, God and the serpent in the Genesis account of the first sin;
• Implement one decision to let God be God.

WARM UP

CREATIVE CREATIONS—
Three questions to help students begin to think about the creation that surrounds them.

TEAM EFFORT— JUNIOR HIGH/ MIDDLE SCHOOL

SCULPTURE CREATIONS—
An activity to help students understand how it feels to create something with their own hands.

TEAM EFFORT— HIGH SCHOOL

IN THE BEGINNING...—
An activity to help students realize the diversity of God's creation.

IN THE WORD

TRACING THE FEELINGS—
A Bible study to explore the human feelings involved in the Genesis story of creation and the curse.

THINGS TO THINK ABOUT (OPTIONAL)

Questions to get students thinking and talking about the nature of the first sin.

PARENT PAGE

A tool to get the session into the home and allow parents and young people to discuss their love for one another in spite of their sins.

THE BOOK OF
GENESIS:
CREATION AND
CURSE

LEADER'S DEVOTION

**"He said to me, 'My grace is sufficient for you, for my power is made perfect in weakness.' Therefore I will boast all the more gladly about my weaknesses, so that Christ's power may rest on me"
(2 Corinthians 12:9).**

I asked God for strength that I might achieve.
I was made weak that I might learn humbly to obey.

I asked God for health that I might do great things.
I was given infirmity that I might do better things.

I asked for riches that I might be happy.
I was given poverty that I might be wise.

I asked for power that I might have the praise of men.
I was given weakness that I might feel the need of God.

I asked for all things that I might enjoy life.
I was given life that I might enjoy all things.

I got nothing I asked for
but everything I had hoped for...

Almost despite myself my unspoken
prayers were answered.

I am among all people most richly blessed.

An unknown confederate soldier wrote these powerful words. Somehow he understood the truth of the above Scripture and the truth behind this session. It is not what you have or even how good you are, but rather Who you know. God created the world, humankind sinned and Christ redeemed us. Our Christian faith is all about God and relying on His strength and not about using our own strength. The apostle Paul wrote it like this:

"The foolishness of God is wiser than man's wisdom, and the weakness of God is stronger than man's strength" (1 Corinthians 1:25).

**"Bring Him your weakness and find strength in His might."
—Jack Hayford**

In your weakest moments, don't be afraid to lean on the strong and steady arms of your Savior. As you introduce your students to this session's description of God's creation, our weakness in sin and the good news of His redemption, please be reminded that like the confederate soldier we are blessed to be used by God despite our imperfections. Isn't God good?

THE BOOK OF GENESIS: CREATION AND CURSE

KEY VERSE

"You will not surely die,' the serpent said to the woman. 'For God knows that when you eat of it your eyes will be opened, and you will be like God, knowing good and evil.'" Genesis 3:4,5

BIBLICAL BASIS

Genesis 2:4—3:19; Matthew 18:21-35; 1 Corinthians 1:25; 10:13; 2 Corinthians 12:9

THE BIG IDEA

We are God's creations, yet because of our sin we have been cursed.

WARM UP (5-10 MINUTES)

CREATIVE CREATIONS

• Divide students into groups of four or five.
• Give each group a copy of "Creative Creations" on page 19, or display a copy using an overhead projector.
• Have students share their answers in their small groups to the following questions:

1. What's the strangest, most bizarre invention you've ever heard of?

....

2. What's the most useful creation or invention you use regularly?

....

3. If you could create or invent anything, what would it be?

....

• If time allows, have each group share their group's best answer to one or more of the questions.

TEAM EFFORT—JUNIOR HIGH/MIDDLE SCHOOL (15-20 Minutes)

SCULPTURE CREATIONS

The goal of this exercise is to help students understand how it feels to create something.

• Divide group into teams of eight members each. Give each student a piece of gum, preferably bubble gum. Have them chew the gum for approximately one minute or until soft and moist.

• Ask each team to spit their individual pieces of gum onto one piece of paper, so that each team has eight pieces of gum on their pieces of paper. Give all teams two minutes to make their most creative sculpture out of their already-chewed gum.

• After two minutes, have each team explain their sculpture.

• Option: If gum seems too disgusting, you may want to use clay or play dough and the groups could be smaller groups of four.

 TEAM EFFORT—HIGH SCHOOL (15-20 Minutes)

IN THE BEGINNING...

The goal of this exercise is to help students recognize the diversity of God's creation.

• Ask for a student volunteer. Give this volunteer a letter of the alphabet and ask him or her to name as many things as he or she can that have been created that begin with that letter. For example, if you give your volunteer the letter F he or she might say "flower," "fly," "fax machines," "flags," etc. The volunteer has 60 seconds to name as many items as possible. It's harder than you might think!

• Repeat with different volunteers and different letters of the alphabet. Give a prize to the student who names the most created things.

IN THE WORD (25-30 Minutes)

TRACING THE FEELINGS

• Give each student a copy of "Tracing the Feelings" on pages 20-21 and a pen or pencil, or display a copy using an overhead projector.

• Explain that today you're going to examine the creation and curse story in Genesis 2 and 3. Perhaps the students are already familiar with the story, but today they're going to examine the feelings of the characters involved.

• Have students take turns reading aloud from Genesis 2:4—3:19. When you get to Genesis 3:1, ask for four volunteers to play the parts of the serpent, Eve, Adam and God and act out what the Scripture says as it is being read.

• Discuss the following questions with the whole group:

Read Genesis 1-3. Discuss the following questions:

1. How do you think Eve felt when God told him he would have a partner?

2. Why would Eve want to be like God?

3. How do you think the serpent must have felt as Eve bit into the forbidden fruit?

4. What do you think Adam and Eve might have been thinking as they were sewing fig leaves together to cover themselves?

5. What would you guess was God's tone of voice in Genesis 3:11?

6. As Adam was explaining to God that it was Eve's fault, how do you think Eve felt?

7. If you were Adam, what would you have wanted to say to Eve after God explained the curse?

8. What would you have wanted to say to Adam if you were Eve?

9. Do you think Adam and Eve were sorry for what they did or sorry that they were caught? Why do you think this?

SO WHAT?

There is a progression in Adam and Eve's feelings about their sin. First it felt good; then they felt ashamed and then they were afraid. Get into pairs to answer the following questions:

1. Think about a temptation in your life. How would giving in to it make you feel good, at least at first?

2. How might giving in to this temptation later make you feel ashamed?

3. Read 1 Corinthians 10:13 aloud. How do you think God may give you a way out of your temptation this week?

 THINGS TO THINK ABOUT (OPTIONAL)

• Use the questions on page 22 after or as a part of "In the Word."

1. Did God know that Adam and Eve would eat from the forbidden tree?

2. Why would God give Adam and Eve a choice in the first place?

3. If Adam and Eve had not sinned, would sin have entered the world?

 PARENT PAGE

• Distribute page to parents.

THE BOOK OF
GENESIS:
CREATION AND
CURSE

CREATIVE CREATIONS

1. What's the strangest, most bizarre invention you've ever heard of?

2. What's the most useful creation or invention you use regularly?

3. If you could create or invent anything, what would it be?

**THE BOOK OF
GENESIS:
CREATION AND
CURSE**

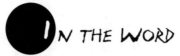

IN THE WORD

TRACING THE FEELINGS

Read Genesis 2—3. Discuss the following questions:

1. How do you think Adam felt when God told him he would have a partner?

2. Why would Eve want to be like God?

3. How do you think the serpent must have felt as Eve bit into the forbidden fruit?

4. What do you think Adam and Eve might have been thinking as they were sewing fig leaves together to cover themselves?

5. What would you guess was God's tone of voice in Genesis 3:11?

6. As Adam was explaining to God that it was Eve's fault, how do you think Eve felt?

7. If you had been Adam, what would you have wanted to say to Eve after God explained the curse?

8. What would you have wanted to say to Adam if you had been Eve?

....
....
....

9. Do you think Adam and Eve were sorry for what they did or sorry that they were caught? Why do you think this?

....
....
....

So What?

We see a progression in Adam and Eve's feelings about their sin. First it felt good, then they felt ashamed and then they were afraid. Get into pairs to answer the following questions:

1. Think about a temptation in your life. How would giving in to it make you feel good, at least at first?

....
....
....

2. How might giving in to this temptation later make you feel ashamed?

....
....
....

3. Read I Corinthians 10:13 aloud. How do you think God may give you a way out of your temptation this week?

....
....
....

THE BOOK OF GENESIS: CREATION AND CURSE

Things to Think About

1. Did God know that Adam and Eve would eat from the forbidden tree?

_____

_____

_____

2. Why would God give Adam and Eve a choice in the first place?

_____

_____

_____

3. If Adam and Eve had not sinned, would sin have entered the world?

_____

_____

_____

 ARENT PAGE

ALL IN THE FAMILY

There's no doubt about it: your family sees you at your worst!

Your family sees you angry, upset or depressed more than anyone else does. As a result, your family members are more likely to be around you when you sin. One important thing is to learn how to respond to another family member when he or she sins against you.

Read Matthew 18:21-35 together as a family. Discuss the following questions.

1. Why is it difficult to continue to forgive someone when they repeatedly sin against you?

2. What was the problem with the servant's attitude and actions?

3. When do we act like the servant in Jesus' parable?

4. What does it mean to "forgive...from your heart" (Matthew 18:35)?

5. How can you make your home a more forgiving environment?

Session 1 "The Book of Genesis: Creation and Curse"

Date

THE BOOK OF EXODUS:
COVENANTS AND COMMANDMENTS

KEY VERSE

"Then Moses went up to God, and the LORD called to him from the mountain and said, 'This is what you are to say to the house of Jacob and what you are to tell the people of Israel: "Now if you obey me fully and keep my covenant, then out of all nations you will be my treasured possession. Although the whole earth is mine, you will be for me a kingdom of priests and a holy nation." ' " Exodus 19:3,5,6

BIBLICAL BASIS

Exodus 19:1-8; 20:1-17;
John 14:21;
Romans 12:10

THE BIG IDEA

God has given commandments to obey to help believers keep their covenant relationship with Him.

AIMS OF THIS SESSION

During this session you will guide students to:
- Examine the covenant relationship with God;
- Discover the Old Testament commandments God wants us to obey;
- Implement one specific way to obey God's commandments.

WARM UP

FOLLOW THE RULES OR ELSE!—

A case study to help students think about the importance of keeping commandments and honoring covenants.

TEAM EFFORT— JUNIOR HIGH/ MIDDLE SCHOOL

SIMON SAYS—

An activity to practice obeying commandments.

TEAM EFFORT— HIGH SCHOOL

IF I WERE A PARENT—

Students put themselves in their parents' shoes.

IN THE WORD

COVENANTS AND COMMANDMENTS—

A Bible study to discover God's covenants and commandments in Exodus.

THINGS TO THINK ABOUT (OPTIONAL)

Questions to get students thinking and talking about the consequences of disobeying God's commands.

PARENT PAGE

A tool to get the session into the home and allow parents and young people to identify the covenants and commandments that operate in their families.

THE BOOK OF EXODUS: COVENANTS AND COMMANDMENTS

LEADER'S DEVOTIONAL

"'Whoever has my commands and obeys them, he is the one who loves me. He who loves me will be loved by my Father, and I too will love him and show myself to him'" (John 14:21).

The Bible isn't a book of magic formulas for a successful life, but these words of Jesus are the key principle for living a victorious Christian life. Just as the book of Exodus was written to give the Israelites commandments and covenants from God, these words of Jesus focus on the same principle: obedience. Basically, Jesus is telling us that the way to show Him we love Him is to obey God's commandments, and the result of obedience and love is that He will reveal Himself to you. Love for God equals obedience (our part) and revelation (God's part).

When it comes to loving others, sometimes it isn't easy to follow God's principles. The world says "Look out for number one!" and "Me first!" The Word says "Love one another with a brotherly affection: outdo one another in showing honor" (Romans 12:10, *RSV*). No one said that living the Christian life would be easy. The following words help give us perspective:

IT IS NOT EASY
To apologize.
To begin over.
To take advice.
To be unselfish.
To admit error.
To face a sneer.
To be charitable.
To keep trying.
To be considerate.
To avoid mistakes.
To endure success.
To profit by mistakes.
To forgive and forget.
To think and then act.
To keep out of a rut.
To make the best of little.
To shoulder a deserved blame.
BUT IT ALWAYS PAYS.
—Anonymous

Obedience to God is always the best way, but most often not the easiest way. God be with you this session as you present these incredible truths to students who need to hear them.

> **"The starting point and the goal of our Christian life is obedience."**
> —Andrew Murray

THE BOOK OF EXODUS: COVENANTS AND COMMANDMENTS

KEY VERSE

"Then Moses went up to God, and the LORD called to him from the mountain and said, 'This is what you are to say to the house of Jacob and what you are to tell the people of Israel: "Now if you obey me fully and keep my covenant, then out of all nations you will be my treasured possession. Although the whole earth is mine, you will be for me a kingdom of priests and a holy nation." '" Exodus 19:3,5,6

BIBLICAL BASIS

Exodus 19:1-8; 20:1-17; John 14:21; Romans 12:10

THE BIG IDEA

God has given commandments to obey to help believers keep their covenant relationship with Him.

WARM UP (5-10 Minutes)

FOLLOW THE RULES, OR ELSE!

• Divide students into groups of three or four.
• Read the following case study to the whole group or give each group a copy of "Follow the Rules, or Else!" on page 29 or display a copy using an overhead projector.
• Discuss the questions.

Kelly's father was just laid off from his job and money was tight around Kelly's house. Since Kelly just received her driver's license, she decided to get a job so she could earn some money to help her family.

At her new job at a fast-food restaurant, her boss asked her to sign an "Employee Covenant" in which she agrees to

---

Fold

---

6. Are God's Old Testament covenants and commandments still as important and relevant today since Jesus has come?

Why or why not?

So What?

Read the commandments chosen by the members in your group and discuss the following:

Which of these commandments is toughest to live out at school?

Pray for each other, asking God to give each of you strength to obey these commandments on your campus(es) this week.

THINGS TO THINK ABOUT (OPTIONAL)

• Use the questions on page 33 after or as a part of "In the Word."

1. Are God's commandments difficult to obey? Why or why not?

2. If we don't obey God's commandments, does God's attitude or feelings toward us change?

3. If someone continually disobeys God's commands but claims to be a Christian, what does this mean?

PARENT PAGE

• Distribute page to parents.

obey the following three rules at the restaurant:
1. She must be on time every day.
2. She must clean the restaurant's dining area regularly.
3. She must be friendly and courteous to her customers.

If she obeys all three rules, she will be promoted and given a raise in salary in one month. Kelly was doing a super job being on time, cleaning the restaurant and being friendly. Two days before her first month was up, Kelly got stuck in traffic and arrived 10 minutes late for her job. Kelly's boss was frustrated. Kelly tried to explain that she got stuck in traffic, but her boss said she had broken the covenant and therefore wouldn't be promoted and wouldn't receive a raise.

1. Was Kelly's boss being fair?

2. If you had been Kelly's boss, what would you you have done?

 TEAM EFFORT—JUNIOR HIGH/MIDDLE SCHOOL (15-20 MINUTES)

Simon Says

Simon Says is a well-known game, but still a favorite with junior highers. Explain that this game of Simon Says is an example of the importance of obeying commands.

• Stand in front of the students and begin to give them commands, such as "Simon says 'Stand up'" or "Simon says 'Put your hands on top of your head.'" Students must follow your commands.

• Periodically give a command, but don't say "Simon says" first. If a student follows the command even though you didn't say "Simon says" he or she is out of the game and must sit down. Students are only to obey commands that begin with "Simon says." The last student remaining in the game wins. (For fun and variety, you may want to change the name of the game by inserting your own name instead of Simon.)

1. If you could abolish one rule at your school, what would it be?

2. Why is it difficult to obey commands that others give you?

TEAM EFFORT—HIGH SCHOOL (15-20 MINUTES)

If I Were a Parent...

The goal of this exercise is to help students decide on the most important commands that a parents should emphasize with their children.

• Ask students which commands or rules they think are most important for parents to teach their children. Write their answers on a chalkboard, whiteboard or an overhead.

• After you have received 10 or so answers, ask students to vote for three commands for Children." Each student can vote for three commands.

1. Why are these the most important commands for parents to give their children?

2. What happens if children do not obey these commands?

 IN THE WORD (25-30 MINUTES)

COVENANTS AND COMMANDMENTS

• Give each student a copy of "Covenants and Commandments" on pages 30-32 and a pen or pencil.

• Divide students into groups of three or four. Have them complete the Bible study up to the "So What?" section.

• Then ask each of the students in the small groups to choose a number from 1 to 10. Then explain that these are the three or four commandments that their small group is going to study together.

• Have students read the three or four commandments that correspond to the numbers chosen by those in their small groups.

• For each commandment, ask students to specify one application that they can implement this week at school.

COVENANT
In the book of Exodus, God clarifies the relationship He wants to have with His followers. Read Exodus 19:1-8 aloud to see what type of relationship God wants.

1. In general, what is a covenant between two people?

2. In verses 3-6, what did God want His people to do?

3. What did God promise to do in return?

4. What does it mean to be "a kingdom of priests and a holy nation"?

5. How does a covenant relationship with God benefit you?

How does it benefit others?

COMMANDMENTS
God gave His people the Ten Commandments to give them specific ways to obey Him. Read Exodus 20:1-17 aloud.

1. Which commandments relate to our relationship with God?

2. Which commandments relate to our relationship with others?

3. Which commandment do you think is the most important?

4. Which commandment is most often broken by non-Christians?

5. Which commandment is broken most often by Christians?

WARM UP

FOLLOW THE RULES OR ELSE!

Kelly's father was just laid off from his job and money was tight around Kelly's house. Since Kelly just received her driver's license, she decided to get a job so she could earn some money to help her family.

At her new job at a fast-food restaurant, her boss asked her to sign an "Employee Covenant" in which she agrees to obey the following three rules at the restaurant:

1. She must be on time every day.
2. She must clean the restaurant's dining area regularly.
3. She must be friendly and courteous to her customers.

If she obeys all three rules, she will be promoted and given a raise in salary in one month.

Kelly was doing a super job being on time, cleaning the restaurant and being friendly. Two days before her first month was up, Kelly got stuck in traffic and arrived 10 minutes late for her job. Kelly's boss was frustrated. Kelly tried to explain that she got stuck in traffic, but her boss said she had broken the covenant and therefore wouldn't be promoted and wouldn't receive a raise.

1. Was Kelly's boss being fair?

2. If you had been Kelly's boss, what would you have done?

THE BOOK OF EXODUS: COVENANTS AND COMMANDMENTS

IN THE WORD

COVENANTS AND COMMANDMENTS

Covenant

In the book of Exodus, God clarifies the relationship He wants to have with His followers. Read Exodus 19:1-8 aloud to see what type of relationship God wants.

1. In general, what is a covenant between two people?

2. In verses 3-6, what did God want His people to do?

3. What did God promise to do in return?

4. What does it mean to be "a kingdom of priests and a holy nation"?

5. How does a covenant relationship with God benefit you?

How does it benefit others?

Commandments

God gave His people the Ten Commandments to give them specific ways to obey Him. Read Exodus 20:1-17 aloud.

1. Which commandments relate to our relationship with God?

2. Which commandments relate to our relationship with others?

3. Which commandment do you think is the most important?

4. Which commandment is broken most often by non-Christians?

5. Which commandment is broken most often by Christians?

6. Are God's Old Testament covenants and commandments still as important and relevant today, since Jesus has come? Why or why not?

**THE BOOK
OF EXODUS:
COVENANTS AND
COMMANDMENTS**

SO WHAT?

Read the commandments chosen by the members in your group and discuss the following:

Which of these commandments is toughest to live out at school?

....

....

....

Pray for one another, asking God to give each of you strength to obey these commandments on your campus(es) this week.

**THE BOOK
OF EXODUS:
COVENANTS AND
COMMANDMENTS**

THINGS TO THINK ABOUT

1. Are God's commandments difficult to obey? Why or why not?

....

....

....

2. If we don't obey God's commandments, does God's attitude or feelings toward us change?

....

....

....

3. If someone continually disobeys God's commands but claims to be a Christian, what does this mean?

....

....

....

**THE BOOK
OF EXODUS:
COVENANTS AND
COMMANDMENTS**

PARENT PAGE

FAMILY COVENANTS AND COMMANDMENTS

The book of Exodus specifies the type of covenant, or two-sided relationship, that God wants to have with His people. In the book of Exodus, God also gives His followers ten commandments to help them live up to their parts of the covenant. As a family, read Exodus 20:1-17 out loud.

Similarly, every family has its own covenants and commandments, sometimes explicit and other times less spelled out. Examples of covenants include the commitment to respect each others' privacy or to love each other no matter what. Types of commandments include keeping rooms clean and arriving home on time.

1. What are the covenants your family members have made to each other?

2. Are these covenants appropriate or do they expect too much or too little from family members?

3. What are your family's commandments or rules?

4. Which of your family's commandments are similar to the Ten Commandments?

5. Are there any other rules or covenants that should be added or deleted?

Spend five minutes writing all of these covenants and commandments on one piece of paper. Post it on your refrigerator for the next two weeks as a reminder of your family's commitment to one another.

Session 2 "The Book of Exodus:
Covenants and Commandments"
Date

THE BOOK OF PSALMS:
PROBLEMS, PRAYERS AND PRAISES

Key Verse

"Save me, O God, by your name; vindicate me by your might. Hear my prayer, O God; listen to the words of my mouth. Strangers are attacking me; ruthless men seek my life—men without regard for God. Surely God is my help; the LORD is the one who sustains me. Let evil recoil on those who slander me; in your faithfulness destroy them. I will sacrifice a freewill offering to you; I will praise your name, O LORD, for it is good. For he has delivered me from all my troubles, and my eyes have looked in triumph on my foes." Psalm 54:1-7

Biblical Basis

Psalm 22; 31:14; 35:4; 54:1-7; 63:1; 94:5; 109:2; 130:1,2; 140:7; 150:6; 1 Timothy 6:6-8

The Big Idea

In the midst of our problems, our prayers will enable us to praise the Lord.

Aims of This Session

During this session you will guide students to:
- Examine the problems in their lives;
- Discover the appropriate responses of prayer and praise during difficult times;
- Implement an attitude of prayer and praise in response to one specific problem.

Warm Up

Worship Song Ping-Pong—
A high-energy activity to help students think about the variety and importance of worship songs.

Team Effort— Junior High/ Middle School

Psalm Bible Quiz—
A game to help students locate different psalms and decide whether they are a problem, a prayer or a praise.

Team Effort— High School

The Paper Chase—
Students practice using prayer and praise as the two best responses when faced with a problem.

In the Word

Problems, Prayers and Praises—
A Bible study to discover the psalmists' models of responding to a problem with prayer and praise.

Things to Think About (OPTIONAL)
Questions to get students thinking and talking about why the psalms have historically been a source of support and encouragement to their readers.

Parent Page

A tool to get the session into the home and allow parents and young people to identify problems in the local or national news that could lead to prayer and praise.

THE BOOK OF
PSALMS:
PROBLEMS,
PRAYERS
AND PRAISES

LEADER'S DEVOTIONAL

"Godliness with contentment is great gain. For we brought nothing into the world, and we can take nothing out of it. But if we have food and clothing, we will be content with that" (1 Timothy 6:6-8).

Cathy and I had the privilege of staying in a wonderful pastor's home in Romania when I was speaking in that country a few years ago. John and his beautiful wife Elizabeth lived in a two-room house with their three children. John was the pastor of a 400-member Baptist church and Elizabeth was a nurse working 12-hour shifts, five nights a week. John made $25 a month and Elizabeth brought home $75. John showed me scars he had on his body from being imprisoned for his faith under the evil rule of Ceausescu.

I looked in the children's cardboard toy box and there was an old model car, a doll with a few strands of hair and some old blocks that looked like they had been found in the trash. I thought back to the closets full of toys in our home. The whole time we were getting ready to eat I looked around the house which, believe me, didn't take a great deal of time. The pastor had four books and his well-worn Bible. The kids slept on a cot and the couch—no beds. The home was what we would call a dump. Their poverty made me feel uncomfortable.

When it was time for dinner, Elizabeth served us, but then didn't eat with us. Cathy thought it was because they didn't have enough food. The meal consisted of a spoonful of sausage and a quarter of a potato. Our water was colored with something red and it had a very foul odor. We drank it, but we just didn't breathe.

As we prepared to eat this terrible-looking sparse meal, our pastor friend grabbed our hands and prayed, "Dear Lord, thank you for our many blessings and thank you for the way you have abundantly provided for us. You are a most gracious and loving God." I sat there stunned, and I must admit, a bit humbled. Here was a man who had been through so much and had so little material goods thanking God for a meal I would have thrown down our garbage disposal. Once again, I was reminded "attitude is everything" and that, as the book of Psalms teaches, even in the midst of trying circumstances there are great reasons to give God praise.

The psalms contain the praises and prayers of the Israelites. It is an honor for those of us in youth work to introduce such powerful and eternally wonderful words of praise to the next generation.

"I complained because I had no shoes until I met a man who had no feet."—Indian proverb

THE BOOK OF PSALMS: PROBLEMS, PRAYERS AND PRAISES

KEY VERSE

"Save me, O God, by your name; vindicate me by your might. Hear my prayer, O God; listen to the words of my mouth. Strangers are attacking me; ruthless men seek my life—men without regard for God. Surely God is my help; the Lord is the one who sustains me. Let evil recoil on those who slander me; in your faithfulness destroy them. I will sacrifice a freewill offering to you; I will praise your name, O Lord, for it is good. For he has delivered me from all my troubles, and my eyes have looked in triumph on my foes." Psalm 54:1-7

BIBLICAL BASIS

Psalm 22; 31:14; 35:4; 54:1-7; 63:1; 94:5; 109:2; 130:1,2; 140:7; 150:6; 1 Timothy 6:6-8

THE BIG IDEA

In the midst of our problems, our prayers will enable us to praise the Lord.

WARM UP (5-10 MINUTES)

WORSHIP SONG PING-PONG

• Divide students by gender. Ask the guys to stand on one side of the room and the girls to stand on the other.

• Explain that today we're going to study the book of Psalms. Many psalms have become parts of worship songs we sing today. Explain that the goal of "Worship Song Ping-Pong" is to come up with more worship songs that are sung at your church or youth ministry than the other team. Ask the guys to begin by singing together the same worship song for five seconds. Then the girls take their turn and also sing together a second worship song for five seconds. The guys should be thinking and discussing together so that when the girls are done, they are ready to sing yet a third song.

• This proceeds back and forth until one side can't think of a worship song, time runs out or they repeat a song that has already been sung.

THINGS TO THINK ABOUT (OPTIONAL)

- Use the questions on page 41 after or as a part of "In the Word."

1. Which psalm has been most meaningful to you? Why?

2. Why do you think many Christians turn to the book of Psalms in times of need?

3. Do you think a non-Christian would also benefit from reading the psalms? Why or why not?

PARENT PAGE

• Distribute page to parents.

TEAM EFFORT—JUNIOR HIGH/MIDDLE SCHOOL (15-20 MINUTES)

PSALM BIBLE QUIZ

- Make sure every student has a Bible. Explain that the object of "Psalm Bible Quiz" is to find the Scripture passage first, stand up and read it aloud so the rest of the group can hear.
- Once the student has read the verse, ask him or her to share with the group whether they think the verse is a problem, a prayer or a praise. (Some of the psalms may be a combination of two of these.)

Work your way through the following verses, one at a time:

Psalm 130:1,2   Psalm 63:1
Psalm 140:7   Psalm 109:2
Psalm 31:14   Psalm 150:6
Psalm 35:4   Psalm 94:5

 TEAM EFFORT—HIGH SCHOOL (15-20 MINUTES)

THE PAPER CHASE

- Divide students into groups of four. Give each group a piece of paper and a pen or pencil. Ask them to write down a description of a typical teenage problem in two to five sentences.
- Have groups switch papers so that now each group has another group's problem. Now ask the groups to write a two to five-sentence prayer below the problem on the paper they received that would be an appropriate response to the problem.
- Have groups switch papers for a final time. Now ask each group to write a two to five-sentence praise that is appropriate to the nature of the problem and the hope of the prayer.

IN THE WORD (25-30 MINUTES)

PROBLEMS, PRAYERS AND PRAISES

- Ask "How do most teenagers respond when faced with a problem?" (You may want to provide discussion starters such as students sleep too much, eat too much or too little, or they run away.) Write their answers on a chalkboard, flipchart or overhead.
- Once you have listed their answers, take a vote to determine "The Top Five Typical Teenage Responses to Problems." Allow each student to vote for two options.
- Explain that many of the 150 psalms written by David and others teach us how we should respond to a problem.
- Give each student a copy of "Problems, Prayers and Praises" on pages 39-40 and a pen or pencil.
- Ask one student to read Psalm 54:1-7 aloud. Explain that this psalm shows us a typical pattern in the psalms.
- Divide students into pairs.
- Ask different pairs to give their answers to the Psalm 54 chart.
- Ask each pair to try to find another psalm that has these three elements and apply the same chart to its contents.

38

Fold

- For the "So What?" section, ask each pair to apply the same elements of the "Problems, Prayers and Praises" section to a situation or dilemma in their own lives.

Many of the 150 psalms written by David and others explain how we should respond to a problem. Complete the following chart with your partner:

PSALM 54

The Problem:
....

The Prayer:
....

The Praise:
....

How was David's attitude at the end of the psalm different from its beginning?
....
....

This pattern in Psalm 54 is fairly common in the book of Psalms. Find another psalm that has these three elements and complete the following chart together:

Psalm ....

The Problem:
....

The Prayer:
....

The Praise:
....

SO WHAT?

With your partner, apply the same elements of problem, prayer and praise to a situation or dilemma in your own lives.

My problem:
....

My prayer:
....

My praise:
....

Take a few moments to pray for each other.

PROBLEMS, PRAYERS AND PRAISES

Many of the 150 psalms written by David and others explain how we should respond to a problem. Complete the following chart with your partner:

Psalm 54

The Problem:

_____

_____

The Prayer:

_____

_____

The Praise:

_____

_____

How was David's attitude at the end of the psalm different from its beginning?

_____

_____

This pattern in Psalm 54 is fairly common in the book of Psalms. Find another psalm that has these three elements and complete the following chart together:

Psalm _____

The Problem:

_____

_____

The Prayer:

_____

_____

THE BOOK OF
PSALMS:
PROBLEMS,
PRAYERS
AND PRAISES

The Praise:

....
....
....

So What?

With your partner, apply the same elements of problem, prayer and praise to a situation or dilemma in your own lives.

My problem:

....
....
....

My prayer:

....
....
....

My praise:

....
....
....

Take a few moments to pray for each other.

THINGS TO THINK ABOUT

1. Which psalm has been most meaningful to you? Why?

....

....

....

2. Why do you think many Christians turn to the book of Psalms in times of need?

....

....

....

3. Do you think a non-Christian would also benefit from reading the psalms? Why or why not?

....

....

....

THE BOOK OF
PSALMS:
PROBLEMS,
PRAYERS
AND PRAISES

PARENT PAGE

A BROADER LOOK

Many of the psalms follow a similar pattern. First, the psalmist begins by specifying a problem. Next, the psalmist responds with prayer. Finally, the psalmist includes a time of praise for God's sovereignty and hope in the midst of difficulties.

Read Psalm 22 aloud. What is the problem facing the writer?

....

....

....

What are the psalmist's specific prayer requests?

....

....

....

How does the psalmist praise God?

....

....

....

As a family, skim the front page of a newspaper, watch news on the television or listen to a news show on the radio.

What is one problem happening in your city or nation today?

....

....

....

How do you want to pray for this particular problem?

....

....

....

How can you praise God in the midst of this problem?

....

....

Session 3 "The Book of Psalms:
Problems, Prayers and Praises"
Date ....

Take a few minutes to pray together as a family for this problem. In the days ahead, pay attention to how God works in this situation. You may want to change your prayer or praise focus as the problem evolves or changes.

THE BOOK OF PROVERBS:
CHOICES AND CONSEQUENCES

KEY VERSE

"The fear of the LORD is the beginning of knowledge, but fools despise wisdom and discipline."
Proverbs 1:7

BIBLICAL BASIS

1 Kings 11:1-13;
Proverbs 1:7,10-33; 3:5-8; 8:13

THE BIG IDEA

Every choice we make, whether foolish or wise, has its consequences.

AIMS OF THIS SESSION

During this session you will guide students to:
• Examine the choices they are making at this particular time in their lives;
• Discover the wisdom that flows from fearing the Lord;
• Implement an understanding of the consequences of positive and negative choices.

WARM UP

HAVE YOU EVER?—
A discussion about choices students have made.

TEAM EFFORT—JUNIOR HIGH/MIDDLE SCHOOL

FLASHBACK—
Students think about the choices they have already made today and the corresponding consequences of those choices.

TEAM EFFORT—HIGH SCHOOL

YES OR NO?—
Four scenarios that force students to make choices and think about consequences.

IN THE WORD

CHOICES AND CONSEQUENCES—
A Bible study on the teachings in Proverbs about wise and foolish choices and their consequences.

THINGS TO THINK ABOUT (OPTIONAL)

Questions to get students thinking and talking about the meaning of the fear of the Lord.

PARENT PAGE

A tool to get the session into the home and allow parents to discuss the consequences of some of their past choices with their young person.

THE BOOK OF
PROVERBS:
CHOICES AND
CONSEQUENCES

LEADER'S DEVOTIONAL

"Trust in the LORD with all your heart and lean not on your own under-standing; in all your ways acknowledge him, and he will make your paths straight. Do not be wise in your own eyes; fear the LORD and shun evil. This will bring health to your body and nourishment to your bones" (Proverbs 3:5-8).

The book of Proverbs warns us of the positive and negative consequences of making choices. I often like to tell students that the decisions they make today will affect them for the rest of their lives. Many of us on the journey of faith do not practice enough wisdom in our lives. The book of Proverbs is loaded with wisdom which, though written thousands of years ago, is still practical for present and future generations.

There is a very old story told about a man in Ireland who was plodding along toward home carrying a huge sack of potatoes. Finally a friend of his came along with a horse and carriage and offered him a ride. The man gladly accepted the ride, but he kept holding the potatoes over his shoulder. His friend suggested that he lighten his burden by laying the bag in the back of the carriage. In a deep Irish brogue the man replied, "I don't like to trouble you too much, sir. You're a givin' me a ride already, so I'll just carry the potatoes!"

It sounds like such a silly decision by this Irish gentleman, but we often do the same thing when it comes to trusting in God. So often we become weary from the heavy load. Instead of giving our burdens to God, we continue to carry the heavy "bag of potatoes" when the Lord's desire is to carry the burden for us. We experience the negative consequences of our foolish choice to bear the burden alone.

It's true some burdens are to be borne, but even those become lighter when we choose to give them over to God and lean on Him.

**"In nature there are neither rewards or punishments— there are only consquences."
—Robert Green Ingersoll**

THE BOOK OF PROVERBS: CHOICES AND CONSEQUENCES

KEY VERSE

"The fear of the LORD is the beginning of knowledge, but fools despise wisdom and discipline." Proverbs 1:7

BIBLICAL BASIS

1 Kings 11:1-13; Proverbs 1:7,10-33; 3:5-8; 8:13

THE BIG IDEA

Every choice we make, whether foolish or wise, has its consequences.

WARM UP (5-10 MINUTES)

Have You Ever?

• Ask students the following questions about choices they have made. After each question, ask if any of the students who answer yes to the following questions would like to share any further details.

• Option: Divide students into groups of three or four and give each group a copy of "Have You Ever?" on page 47, or display a copy using an overhead.

1. Have you ever made a choice that got you into big trouble with your parents?

....

2. Have you ever made a choice that really encouraged a friend?

....

3. Have you ever made a choice that made your brother or sister angry?

....

— Fold —

So What?

• Divide your students into groups of three and have them answer the following questions together.

You make choices all the time, some big and some little. With your group, discuss your answers to the following questions:

1. What is this biggest choice you are facing this week?

....

2. What would be a foolish option to choose in this situation?

....

3. What would be the consequences of this foolish choice?

....

4. What would be a wise choice to make in this situation?

....

5. What would be its consequences?

....

6. What will you choose to do?

....

THINGS TO THINK ABOUT (OPTIONAL)

• Use the questions on page 51 after or as a part of "In the Word."

1. Why would a loving God also want us to fear Him?

....

2. Is there a difference between the fear of God and the fear of heights or snakes? If so, what?

....

3. Do you fear anything or anyone more than God? Why?

....

PARENT PAGE

• Distribute page to parents.

TEAM EFFORT—JUNIOR HIGH/MIDDLE SCHOOL (15-20 MINUTES)

FLASHBACK

- Explain that each of us makes choices all the time, sometimes without even realizing it. Even when we do not make a conscious choice, we are making a choice nonetheless.
- Ask students to share a choice they have already made today and its consequences. You may need to start the discussion with choices such as waking up so that you could be here with us today; brushing your teeth to prevent tooth decay and bad breath and so on.

Are there any choices that have no consequences?

TEAM EFFORT—HIGH SCHOOL (15-20 MINUTES)

YES OR NO?

- Place one sign that says Yes on one wall; place a second sign that says No on the opposite wall. Ask students to make a choice about how they would respond in the following case studies and move to the corresponding wall. There is no neutral position; students must choose Yes or No.
- After students have made their choices and are standing next to a wall, ask a few of them to explain their decisions with special attention given to the consequences of the choice.

Case Study #1: Your friend Krista is dating Greg. You know she really likes him. Another friend, Lisa, tells you that Greg has been flirting with her when Krista is not around. Should you tell Krista what Lisa has told you?

Case Study #2: You and a bunch of friends are hanging out at Tom's house, waiting for another friend to arrive so you can all go out together for dinner. As you are waiting, someone suggests that you skip dinner and head for the new R-rated movie that has its grand opening that night. The rest of the group agrees that it's a good idea. You remain silent because you've told your parents that you are going to dinner only, and you know they would not approve of this movie because it's rated R. Would you go anyway?

Case Study #3: You notice your friend Sally is losing a lot of weight. You know that her cheerleading advisor is putting her under a lot of stress, so you ask her if there's anything wrong. Sally says, "Will you promise not to tell anyone?"

You answer, "Sure."

Sally continues, "Well, I think I'm developing an eating disorder. I haven't told anyone yet, not even my parents. You're the first person I've told."

You know Sally's parents and think they'd understand and not freak out, but you've told Sally you wouldn't tell anyone. Knowing that eating disorders are life-threatening, should you tell Sally's parents even though you've promised not to tell?

Are there any choices that have no consequences?

 IN THE WORD (25-30 MINUTES)

CHOICES AND CONSEQUENCES

- Give each student a copy of "Choices and Consequences" on pages 48-50 and a pen or pencil, or display a copy using an overhead projector.
- With the whole group, read and discuss the following:

The book of Proverbs written largely by Solomon, David's son, is full of statements that warn us of the consequences of our choices. Today we're going to look at the first chapter to see what it teaches about choices and consequences.
Read Proverbs 1:10-19 aloud.

1. **What choices are described in this passage?**

2. **What are the consequences of these choices?**

Read Proverbs 1:20-32 aloud.

3. **How are the choices and consequences in this passage similar to those in Proverbs 1:10-19?**

Read Proverbs 1:33 aloud.

4. **What is the choice made in this verse?**

5. **How are the consequences in 1:33 different from the consequences we have already discussed?**

The key to all choices is explained in Proverbs 1:7.
6. **What does it mean to "fear the Lord?" For help in answering this question, read Proverbs 8:13.**

(You may also need to explain that "the fear of God" means acknowledging that there is only one God, Creator and Sustainer of everything and that we are accountable to Him for every choice we make. Therefore, to "fear God" means to love and respect Him. This kind of fear is something like the respect that some students may have for their parents except on a larger scale.)

Let's see if Solomon lived out his own advice. Read 1 Kings 11:1-13 aloud.
7. **What distracted Solomon?**

8. **How do you think God felt as He described to Solomon the consequences of his choices?**

WARM UP

HAVE YOU EVER?

1. Have you ever made a choice that got you into big trouble with your parents?

....

....

....

2. Have you ever made a choice that really encouraged a friend?

....

....

....

3. Have you ever made a choice that made your brother or sister angry?

....

....

....

THE BOOK OF
PROVERBS:
CHOICES AND
CONSEQUENCES

IN THE WORD

CHOICES AND CONSEQUENCES

The book of Proverbs written largely by Solomon, David's son, is full of statements that warn us of the consequences of our choices. Today we're going to look at the first chapter to see what it teaches about choices and consequences.

Read Proverbs 1:10-19 aloud.

1. What choices are described in this passage?

2. What are the consequences of these choices?

Read Proverbs 1:20-32 aloud.

3. How are the choices and consequences in this passage similar to those in Proverbs 1:10-19?

Read Proverbs 1:33 aloud.

4. What is the choice made in this verse?

5. How are the consequences in 1:33 different from the consequences we have already discussed?

The key to all choices is explained in Proverbs 1:7.

6. What does it mean to "fear the Lord"? For help in answering this question, read Proverbs 8:13.

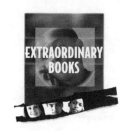

Let's see if Solomon lived out his own advice. Have a student read 1 Kings 11:1-13 aloud.

7. What distracted Solomon?

....

....

....

8. How do you think God felt as He described to Solomon the consequences of his choices?

....

....

So What?

You make choices all the time, some big and some little. With your group, discuss your answers to the following questions:

1. What is the biggest choice you are facing this week?

....

....

....

2. What would be a foolish option to choose in this situation?

....

....

....

3. What would be the consequences of this foolish choice?

....

....

....

4. What would be a wise choice to make in this situation?

....

....

....

5. What would be its consequences?

....
....
....

6. What will you choose to do?

....
....
....

SESSION FOUR

THE BOOK OF PROVERBS: CHOICES AND CONSEQUENCES

Things to Think About

1. Why would a loving God also want us to fear Him?

2. Is there a difference between the fear of God and the fear of heights or snakes? If so, what?

3. Do you fear anything or anyone more than God? Why?

51 © 1996 by Gospel Light. Permission to photocopy granted.

**THE BOOK OF
PROVERBS:
CHOICES AND
CONSEQUENCES**

PARENT PAGE

LEARNING FROM THE CHOICES OF OTHERS

Often students are surprised to find out about some of the bad choices their parents made when they were teenagers.

Questions for the student to ask the parent:

1. What is one of the worst choices you made when you were a teenager?

2. Why did you make this choice?

3. What were the consequences of this choice?

4. If you had to do it all over again, how would you change your choice?

Questions for the parent to ask the student:

1. How does hearing about this choice change your view of me?

2. How do you know if a choice is right or not? Read Proverbs 1:7 together and see how its contents help you answer this question.

3. How can I help you make right choices?

....

....

....

4. What is one specific choice you face that you would like me to pray about?

....

....

....

Take a few minutes to pray together that God would guide in this important choice. As a parent, try to ask how your teen is doing in making this choice in a few days.

Session 4 "The Book of Proverbs: Choices
and Consequences"
Date ....

OUR EXTRAORDINARY GOD

LEADER'S PEP TALK

"When I was a teenager, I used to view God as a bank president. He looked fifty-five years old, sat behind a huge mahogany desk and wore a three-piece suit. I had to come to Him with my requests and needs, just hoping that He would approve them."

This comment from a youth worker friend of mine provoked my thinking. How do the students who sit in front of me week after week view God?

As a bank president?

As a Santa Claus, jolly and happy, ready to give good gifts?

As an old, frail grandfather?

As a combination of all three?

If we were to dive into the brains of our students, I think we would be surprised—and scared—at how little they truly know about God.

The images of God in the Old Testament help wipe the smudges off the lenses through which we view Him.

He is the Creator...

The Provider...

The Pillar of Cloud by day and Fire by night...

The Miracle Worker...

The great "I Am"...

The Holy One...

The Shepherd...

The Father...

This unit has been designed to help you steer your students past the false views they may have of God in order to see how extraordinary He truly is. A fulfilling relationship with God is impossible apart from an understanding of His true nature. Anything less leaves our students (and ourselves!) limping along the path toward growth.

Please be in prayer that God would reveal Himself—His Extraordinary Self—to your students as you study these four sessions together.

A GOD WHO KEEPS HIS PROMISES

KEY VERSES

"Abraham believed the LORD, and he credited it to him as righteousness."
Genesis 15:6

BIBLICAL BASIS

Genesis 12:1-5; 15:6; 17:15-17;
18:1-15; 21:1-7;
Deuteronomy 31:7,8;
Nehemiah 8:10;
Psalm 103:17; 130:3,4;
Isaiah 54:10;
Jeremiah 29:11;
Matthew 28:20;
John 3:16; 14:26; 16:13,24;
Acts 10:43;
Ephesians 3:12; 6:1-4;
Philippians 1:6;
Hebrews 13:5;
1 John 1:9

THE BIG IDEA

Our God keeps His promises to us.

AIMS OF THIS SESSION

During this session you will guide students to:
- Examine the promises God made and kept with Abraham;
- Discover the obstacles that prevent students from trusting in God's promises;
- Implement one way to live according to God's promises.

WARM UP

WHO WOULD KEEP A PROMISE?—
A comparison of types of people who make and often break promises.

TEAM EFFORT— JUNIOR HIGH/ MIDDLE SCHOOL

DESCRIBING OUR EXTRAORDINARY GOD—
A chance for students to examine their initial concepts of God.

TEAM EFFORT— HIGH SCHOOL

A BROKEN PROMISE—
A search into the ways that breaking promises hurts others.

IN THE WORD

PROMISES, PROMISES...—
A Bible study about the God who kept His promises to Abraham.

THINGS TO THINK ABOUT (OPTIONAL)

Questions to get students thinking and talking about God's timing in fulfilling His promises.

PARENT PAGE

A tool to get the session into the home and allow parents and young people to look at the importance of keeping promises in a healthy and happy family.

LEADER'S DEVOTIONAL

"'Be strong and courageous....The LORD himself goes before you and will be with you; he will never leave you nor forsake you. Do not be afraid; do not be discouraged'" (Deuteronomy 31:7,8).

As the title of this chapter reads, God keeps His promises. A promise is a vow, a declaration or a pledge. Did you know that there are over three thousand promises in the Bible? God's promises are words we can trust and in them we can find great comfort. Over the years I have created a small list of promises from God which are close to my heart. Often I read them when I am down, tired, drained or simply in need of a wonderful reminder of God's faithfulness. The following are words of strength and promises for you:

Promises of His Unfailing Love

"'Though the mountains be shaken and the hills be removed, yet my unfailing love for you will not be shaken nor my covenant of peace be removed,' says the Lord, who has compassion on you" (Isaiah 54:10).

"'For God so loved the world that he gave his one and only son, that whoever believes in him shall not perish but have eternal life'" (John 3:16).

Promises of His Forgiveness

"If we confess our sins, he is faithful and just and will forgive us our sins and purify us from all unrighteousness" (1 John 1:9).

"All the prophets testify about him that everyone who believes in him receives forgiveness of sins through his name" (Acts 10:43).

Promises of His Comfort

"But from everlasting to everlasting the Lord's love is with those who fear him, and his righteousness with their children's children" (Psalm 103:17).

"'And surely I am with you always, to the very end of the age'" (Matthew 28:20).

Promises of His Guidance

"'But the Counselor, the Holy Spirit, whom the Father will send in my name, will teach you all things and will remind you of everything I have said to you'" (John 14:26).

"But when he, the Spirit of truth, comes, he will guide you into all truth. He will not speak on his own; he will speak only what he hears, and he will tell you what is yet to come" (John 16:13).

Promises of His Joy

"Nehemiah said, 'Go and enjoy choice food and sweet drinks, and send some to those who have nothing prepared. This day is sacred to our Lord. Do not grieve, for the joy of the Lord is your strength'" (Nehemiah 8:10).

"Until now you have not asked for anything in my name. Ask and you will receive, and your joy will be complete" (John 16:24).

Promises of Freedom from Guilt

"In him and through faith in him we may approach God with freedom and confidence" (Ephesians 3:12).

"If you, O Lord, kept a record of sins, O Lord, who could stand? But with you there is forgiveness; therefore you are feared" (Psalm 130:3,4).

"God don't sponsor no flops!"—Ethel Waters

A GOD WHO KEEPS HIS PROMISES

KEY VERSES

"Abraham believed the LORD, and he credited it to him as righteousness." Genesis 15:6

BIBLICAL BASIS

Genesis 12:1-5; 15:6; 17:15-17; 18:1-15; 21:1-7; Deuteronomy 31:7,8; Nehemiah 8:10; Psalm 103:17; 130:3,4; Isaiah 54:10; Jeremiah 29:11; Matthew 28:20; John 3:16; 14:26; 16:13,24; Acts 10:43; Ephesians 3:12; 6:1-4; Philippians 1:6; Hebrews 13:5; 1 John 1:9

THE BIG IDEA

Our God keeps His promises to us.

WARM UP (5-10 MINUTES)

WHO WOULD KEEP A PROMISE?

• Discuss the following with the whole group:
Which of these people do you think would keep a promise?
A politician who promises to act in the interest of the voters, and not in his or her own best interests.
A close friend who promises that he (or she) won't tell anyone that you want to break up with your girlfriend (or boyfriend).
A parent who promises to leave work early to come to your basketball game.
A television reporter who promises to tell the whole truth and nothing but the truth.
A school teacher who promises that the final exam will be easy.
Which of these five people do you think would be the *best* promise keeper? Explain your answer.

Fold

THINGS TO THINK ABOUT (OPTIONAL)

• Use the questions on page 64 after or as a part of "In the Word."

1. **Do you think God ever delays in fulfilling His promises?**

2. **When God doesn't seem to be fulfilling His promises in the way we want Him to, what should we do?**

3. **How can you encourage a friend who is doubting whether God will keep His promises?**

PARENT PAGE

• Distribute page to parents.

DESCRIBING OUR EXTRAORDINARY GOD

• Discuss the first question with the whole group.
• Divide students into pairs and give each of them a copy of "Describing Our Extraordinary God" on page 59 or display a copy on an overhead projector.
• Have them discuss the remaining questions.

It's been said that every problem we have that causes us to lose our hope, faith or joy relates to our concept of God.

Do you think this statement is true or false? Why or why not?

Discuss the following questions:

1. What specific problem are you dealing with right now?

....

2. How do your actions and thoughts concerning this problem relate to your concept of God?

....

3. If you were given 30 seconds to describe God, what would you say?

....

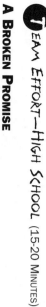

TEAM EFFORT—HIGH SCHOOL (15-20 MINUTES)

A BROKEN PROMISE

• Divide students into groups of three or four.
• Give each student a copy of "A Broken Promise" on page 60 or display it on an overhead projector.
• Have the small groups discuss the questions.

It was the third quarter of the homecoming football game. Mike, one of the defensive linemen, was sitting on the bench peering anxiously into the crowd. His dad had promised to come to the game. After all, Mike was a senior; this was his dad's last chance to see him in action. Mike knew that his dad had an important business appointment that afternoon, but he had hoped that his dad would keep his promise. Mike hoped in vain. His dad never made it to the game.

1. What is wrong with Mike's dad making a promise that he didn't keep?

....

2. Who is Mike's dad hurting by breaking these promises?

....

3. What would you want to say to Mike?

....

4. If you had the opportunity, what would you want to say to Mike's dad?

....

IN THE WORD (25-30 MINUTES)

PROMISES, PROMISES...

• Divide students into groups of three or four.
• Give each student a copy of "Promises, Promises..." on pages 61-63, or display a copy using an overhead projector.

Fold

• Have students complete the study.

Although God has an infinite number of extraordinary qualities, today we are going to study just one of those qualities: He is a promise-keeping God. This is especially seen in His faithfulness in His promises to Abraham.

1. Read Genesis 12:1-5. What are the promises God made to Abraham?

....

2. How did Abraham respond to God's promises and commands?

....

At the heart of God's promises to Abraham was His promise that Abraham would have many descendants and that through those descendants all the families of the earth would be blessed. But Abraham and Sarah had one major problem: they were getting older and still they had no children. Abraham was 100 years old and Sarah was 90 years old—far from the ideal childbearing age (see Genesis 17:15-17)!

3. Read Genesis 18:1-15. What did the Lord promise to Abraham and Sarah?

How did Sarah respond?

....

4. Explain Genesis 18:13,14 in your own words.

....

5. Read Genesis 21:1-7. If you had been a friend of Abraham and Sarah's, what would you have told them as they proudly showed baby Isaac to you for the first time?

....

6. What do you think Abraham would say to anyone who doubts that God will keep His promises?

....

SO WHAT?

1. Summarize God's promises to you in each of these passages:

Jeremiah 29:11

John 3:16

Philippians 1:6

Hebrews 13:5

2. Which promise is most meaningful to you today?

....

3. How can you live according to that promise this week?

....

4. What prevents you from trusting in God's promises?

....

5. What can you do to overcome this obstacle?

....

TEAM EFFORT

DESCRIBING OUR EXTRAORDINARY GOD

Discuss the following:

1. What specific problem are you dealing with right now?

....

....

....

2. How do your actions and thoughts concerning this problem relate to your concept of God?

....

....

....

3. If you were given 30 seconds to describe God, what would you say?

....

....

....

A GOD
WHO KEEPS
HIS PROMISES

TEAM EFFORT

A BROKEN PROMISE

It was the third quarter of the homecoming football game. Mike, one of the defensive linemen, was sitting on the bench peering anxiously into the crowd. His dad had promised to come to the game. After all, Mike was a senior; this was his dad's last chance to see him in action. Mike knew that his dad had an important business appointment that afternoon, but he had hoped that his dad would keep his promise.

Mike hoped in vain. His dad never made it to the game.

1. What is wrong with Mike's dad making a promise that he didn't keep?

....
....
....

2. Who is Mike's dad hurting by breaking these promises?

....
....
....

3. What would you want to say to Mike?

....
....
....

4. If you had the opportunity, what would you want to say to Mike's dad?

....
....
....

A GOD
WHO KEEPS
HIS PROMISES

PROMISES, PROMISES...

Although God has an infinite number of extraordinary qualities, today we are going to study just one of those qualities: He is a promise-keeping God. This is especially seen in His faithfulness in His promises to Abraham.

1. Read Genesis 12:1-5. What were the promises God made to Abraham?

_____

_____

_____

2. How did Abraham respond to God's promises and commands?

_____

_____

_____

At the heart of God's promises to Abraham was His promise that Abraham would have many descendants and that through those descendants all the families of the earth would be blessed. But Abraham and Sarah had one major problem: they were getting older and still they had no children. Abraham was 100 years old and Sarah was 90 years old—far from the ideal childbearing age (see Genesis 17:15-17)!

3. Read Genesis 18:1-15. What did the Lord promise to Abraham and Sarah?

_____

_____

_____

How did Sarah respond?

_____

_____

_____

4. Explain Genesis 18:13,14 in your own words.

_____

_____

_____

A GOD
WHO KEEPS
HIS PROMISES

5. Read Genesis 21:1-7. If you had been a friend of Abraham and Sarah's, what would you have told them as they proudly showed baby Isaac to you for the first time?

....
....
....

6. What do you think Abraham would say to anyone who doubts that God will keep His promises?

....
....

SO WHAT?

1. Summarize God's promises to you in each of the following passages:

....
....

Jeremiah 29:11

....
....

John 3:16

....
....

Philippians 1:6

....
....

Hebrews 13:5

....
....

2. Which promise is most meaningful to you today?

....
....
....

3. How can you live according to that promise this week?

....
....
....

4. What prevents you from trusting in God's promises?

....
....
....

5. What can you do to overcome this obstacle?

....
....
....

A GOD
WHO KEEPS
HIS PROMISES

THINGS TO THINK ABOUT

1. Do you think God ever delays in fulfilling His promises?

....

....

....

2. When God doesn't seem to be fulfilling His promises in the way we want Him to, what should we do?

....

....

....

3. How can you encourage a friend who is doubting whether God will keep His promises?

....

....

....

A GOD
WHO KEEPS
HIS PROMISES

POINTING OUT THE PROMISES

Promises are at the very heart of any relationship, including family relationships. Although we may not be aware of these promises, they nonetheless become the skeleton that holds any family together.

On a scale of 1 to 5—1 being the lowest, 5 being the highest—rank how important these promises are to the health of your family.

Promises that students make:

_____ To keep their rooms clean.

_____ To share with their parents about their day.

_____ To tell the truth about their plans for the weekend.

Promises that parents make:

_____ To pray for the student.

_____ To be interested and ask questions about their day.

_____ To trust the student's judgment.

What other promises are part of the skeleton that holds your family together?

....

....

....

What happens to your family when these promises are not kept?

....

....

....

What role does trust play in making and believing promises?

....

....

....

A GOD
WHO KEEPS
HIS PROMISES

Read Ephesians 6:1-4 aloud together as a family. What is the promise God gives to children if they honor their fathers and mothers?

....

....

....

What can you do this month to try to keep the promises you've made to other family members?

....

....

....

Session 5 "A God Who Keeps His
Promises"   Date ....

A GOD WHO OPPOSES SIN

KEY VERSES

"The LORD said to Joshua, 'Stand up! What are you doing down on your face? Israel has sinned; they have violated my covenant, which I commanded them to keep. They have taken some of the devoted things; they have stolen, they have lied, they have put them with their own possessions. That is why the Israelites cannot stand against their enemies; they turn their backs and run because they have been made liable to destruction. I will not be with you anymore unless you destroy whatever among you is devoted to destruction.'"
Joshua 7:10-12

BIBLICAL BASIS

Joshua 7:1-26;
Proverbs 6:16-19;
Romans 3:23; 5:8

THE BIG IDEA

Our God opposes sin, but He still loves us!

AIMS OF THIS SESSION

During this session you will guide students to:
• Examine the strong opposition God has toward sin.
• Discover the reason why God so strongly opposes sin.
• Implement a plan to hold each other accountable for avoiding sin.

WARM UP

A COMMON LOATHING—
Students identify things that they hate.

TEAM EFFORT—JUNIOR HIGH/MIDDLE SCHOOL

WHAT BUGS GOD?—
An activity that tries to answer the question "What bugs God?"

TEAM EFFORT—HIGH SCHOOL

YOU BE THE JUDGE—
Students determine the appropriate punishment for teens who get into trouble.

IN THE WORD

WHY? WHY? WHY?—
A Bible study that examines the reasons people sin and the reasons God hates sin.

THINGS TO THINK ABOUT (OPTIONAL)

Questions to get students thinking and talking about God's opposition to sin.

PARENT PAGE

A tool to get the session into the home and allow parents and young people to discover how God's opposition to sin is coupled with His mercy.

A GOD WHO
OPPOSES SIN

LEADER'S DEVOTIONAL

"But God demonstrates his own love for us in this: While we were still sinners, Christ died for us" (Romans 5:8).

There is a scene from the movie *Chariots of Fire* that is forever embedded in my mind. Eric Liddell went to the 1924 Olympics in Paris, France. He was assigned to run the 100-yard dash on Sunday. There was only one thing this incredible athlete took more seriously than his running, and that was his faith. For Liddell, his faith told him he could not run on Sunday. All efforts to persuade him otherwise failed. A British dignitary finally cried out in frustration "What a pity we couldn't have persuaded him to run." After a moment's pause his coach responded, "It would have been a pity if we had, because we would have separated him from the source of his speed." Eric Liddell's obedience to God was his source of strength and purpose. His firm stand for God helped him to be one of the most inspiring athletes of the twentieth century.

God doesn't oppose sin because He is the great killjoy, but rather because He knows that sin keeps us from our source of power to live the Christian life. How about you? Is your desire to serve Jesus greater than any of your other desires? This session is a good time to take another look at your own priorities. I've never met a person who put God first in his or her life and ever regretted it.

"I don't know what the future holds, but I know who holds the future."
—E. Stanley Jones

A GOD WHO OPPOSES SIN

![K] EY VERSES

"The LORD said to Joshua, 'Stand up! What are you doing down on your face? Israel has sinned; they have violated my covenant, which I commanded them to keep. They have taken some of the devoted things; they have stolen, they have lied, they have put them with their own possessions. That is why the Israelites cannot stand against their enemies; they turn their backs and run because they have been made liable to destruction. I will not be with you any-more unless you destroy whatever among you is devoted to destruction.'" Joshua 7:10-12

![B] IBLICAL BASIS

Joshua 7:1-26; Proverbs 6:16-19; Romans 3:23; 5:8

![T] HE BIG IDEA

Our God opposes sin, but He still loves us!

![W] ARM UP (5-10 MINUTES)

A COMMON LOATHING

• Divide students into groups of three. Give each group a piece of paper and a pen or pencil.
• Have them work together in their groups to make a list of all the things that all three group members hate (it's important to stress *things*, not people). Such things might include home-work, broccoli and waking up early in the morning.
• Give each group four minutes to complete its list. After the time is up, have each group read its list. You may want to give a prize or special recognition to the group that compiles the longest list.

![T] HINGS TO THINK ABOUT (OPTIONAL)

• Use the questions on page 73 after or as a part of "In the Word."
1. Given your own personal struggles with sin, what do you think are some of the factors that cause a person to sin?

2. Does God always withdraw His blessings from our lives when we sin (as He did with Israel because of Achan's sin)? Why or why not?

3. Perhaps you've heard the phrase "God hates sin, but He loves sinners." How would you explain to a ten-year-old what that phrase means?

![P] ARENT PAGE

• Distribute page to parents.

Fold

Team Effort—Junior High/Middle School (15-20 Minutes)

What Bugs God?

- Combine two of each of the three member groups from the "Warm Up" activity into groups of six students each. Give each group a piece of paper and a pen or pencil.
- Ask each group to come up with a list of all the things they can think of that might bug God. Explain that they will receive one point for each item on their lists and an additional five points if they can come up with Scripture references that support their lists.
- After a few minutes, have each group share its list, noting similarities and differences between the lists. Give a simple prize to the group with the highest score.

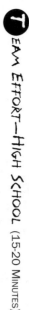

Team Effort—High School (15-20 Minutes)

You Be the Judge

- Combine two of each of the three member groups from the "Warm Up" activity into groups of six students each. Give each group a piece of paper and a pen or pencil.
- Ask each group to work together to come up with a scenario in which a high school student gets into trouble. Scenarios may include cheating on a test, being late for curfew, or spending too much time on the phone (or all three!). The more creative, the better!
- Once the groups have finished writing down their scenarios, have them switch scenarios with another group. Have each group decide on the consequences for the teen in trouble.
- After a few minutes, have the groups share the scenario they were given as well as the consequences for the teenager.

Why? Why? Why?

- Give each student a copy of "Why? Why? Why?" on pages 71-72 and a pen or pencil, or display a copy using an overhead projector.
- Discuss the following with the whole class.

Although God loves us, He does not like it when we sin. Our sin reveals our disobedience and our desire to rule our own lives, instead of letting God rule our lives.

Read Joshua 7:1-26 to see how all of Israel got in trouble because of God's opposition to sin. This passage provokes several questions, all of which begin with the word "why."

1. Why did God's anger burn in Joshua 7:1?

2. Why did Israel lose the battle at Ai in Joshua 7:2-12?

3. Why was it important for the Israelites to consecrate themselves in Joshua 7:13-18?

4. Why did Achan take some of the riches from Ai as described in Joshua 7:19-24?

....

5. Why would God want Achan killed?

6. Why did the Israelites also kill Achan's children and animals?

7. Why did God allow all of Israel to suffer for only one person's sin?

So What?

- Have students find a partner to discuss the following questions with. Ask them to give answers that are honest and are to be kept confidential. Before asking them the following questions, explain that sin can be defined as "missing the mark."

Discuss the following questions with your partner. Give answers that are honest and are to be kept confidential. Remember that sin can be defined as "missing the mark." In other words, we miss out on God's target, or intentions, for us because of our own disobedience and poor choices.

1. Why don't teenagers, in general, hate sin?

2. What is one common sin teenagers often fall into?

3. In what areas are you personally missing the mark?

4. When can the two of you talk again to hold yourselves accountable for taking a step to avoid missing the mark?

....

Fold

In the Word (25-30 Minutes)

IN THE WORD

WHY? WHY? WHY?

Although God loves us, He does not like it when we sin. Our sin reveals our disobedience and our desire to rule our own lives, instead of letting God rule our lives.

Read Joshua 7:1-26 to see how all of Israel got in trouble because of God's opposition to sin. This passage provokes several questions, all of which begin with the word "why."

1. Why did God's anger burn in Joshua 7:1?

_____

_____

_____

2. Why did Israel lose the battle at Ai in Joshua 7:2-12?

_____

_____

_____

3. Why was it important for the Israelites to consecrate themselves in Joshua 7:13-18?

_____

_____

_____

4. Why did Achan take some of the riches from Ai as described in Joshua 7:19-24?

_____

_____

_____

5. Why would God want Achan killed?

_____

_____

_____

6. Why did the Israelites also kill Achan's children and animals?

_____

_____

_____

7. Why did God allow all of Israel to suffer for only one person's sin?

....

....

So What?

Discuss the following questions with your partner. Give answers that are honest and are to be kept confidential. Remember that sin can be defined as "missing the mark." In other words, we miss out on God's target, or intentions, for us because of our own disobedience and poor choices.

1. Why don't teenagers, in general, hate sin?

....

....

....

2. What is one common sin teenagers often fall into?

....

....

....

3. In what areas are you personally missing the mark?

....

....

....

4. When can the two of you talk again to hold yourselves accountable for taking a step to avoid missing the mark?

....

....

....

THINGS TO THINK ABOUT

1. Given your own personal struggles with sin, what do you think are some of the factors that cause a person to sin?

....

....

....

2. Does God always withdraw His blessings from our lives when we sin (as He did with Israel because of Achan's sin)? Why or why not?

....

....

....

3. Perhaps you've heard the phrase "God hates sin, but He loves sinners." How would you explain to a ten-year-old what that phrase means?

....

....

....

A GOD WHO
OPPOSES SIN

PARENT PAGE

THE GOOD NEWS

The Bible teaches in Romans 3:23, "All have sinned and fall short of the glory of God." God hates sin, as clearly explained in Proverbs 6:16-19. Have one family member read the Proverbs passage aloud.

1. How would you rewrite these seven sins in today's language?

....

....

....

2. What are some current examples of these seven sins in family relationships today?

....

....

....

3. Which of these seven sins does your family unfortunately demonstrate most often?

....

....

....

4. Why do you think these listed sins are so detestable to God?

....

....

The word "mercy" means God's unmerited favor. In other words, He acts kindly toward us even when we don't deserve it.

5. What is one example from your own life when you know God was both opposing your sin and being merciful to you at the same time?

....

....

....

Take time as a family to pray, thanking God for His mercy to you even in the midst of your sin.

Session 6: "A God Who Opposes Sin"
Date ....

A GOD WHO WORKS MIRACLES

KEY VERSE

"At the time of sacrifice, the prophet Elijah stepped forward and prayed, 'O LORD, God of Abraham, Isaac and Israel, let it be known today that you are God in Israel and that I am your servant and have done all these things at your command. Answer me, O LORD, answer me, so these people will know that you, O LORD, are God, and that you are turning their hearts back again.'

"Then the fire of the LORD fell and burned up the sacrifice, the wood, the stones and the soil, and also licked up the water in the trench.

"When all the people saw this, they fell prostrate and cried, 'The LORD—he is God! The LORD—he is God!' " 1 Kings 18:36-39

BIBLICAL BASIS

1 Kings 17:1,17-24; 18:16-46; John 10:31,32,37,38

THE BIG IDEA

Our God is powerful and works countless miracles.

AIMS OF THIS SESSION

During this session you will guide students to:
• Examine God's miracles in the life of Elijah;
• Discover God's power to work miracles in their lives;
• Implement prayer groups to ask God for big things.

WARM UP

DYNAMIC DUOS—

An activity to help students get to know one another better.

TEAM EFFORT— JUNIOR HIGH/ MIDDLE SCHOOL

YOU WON'T BELIEVE WHAT GOD DID!—

Students try to remember God's amazing acts throughout the Old Testament.

TEAM EFFORT— HIGH SCHOOL

MIRACLES THEN AND NOW—

A comparison of God's miracles in the Old Testament with God's miracles in their own lives.

IN THE WORD

THREE MAJOR MIRACLES—

A Bible study examining three major miracles in Elijah's life.

THINGS TO THINK ABOUT (OPTIONAL)

Questions to get students thinking and talking about why God chooses to perform miracles at some times but not others.

PARENT PAGE

A tool to get the session into the home and allow parents and young people to begin to pray specifically for one another and for their families.

A GOD WHO
WORKS MIRACLES

LEADER'S DEVOTIONAL

"Again the Jews picked up stones to stone him, but Jesus said to them, 'I have shown you many great miracles from the Father. For which of these do you stone me? Do not believe me unless I do what my Father does. But if I do it, even though you do not believe me, believe the miracles, that you may know and understand that the Father is in me, and I in the Father'" (John 10:31,32,37,38).

Do you believe in miracles? I do. I don't believe that everything called a miracle really is a miracle. In fact, I've been disappointed more than once with something or someone who faked a miracle. Yet miracles happen all around us every day. Some of the miracles are extraordinary; others, like a sunset, the human body or the true love of a man and woman, have become so ordinary that we hardly call them a miracle even though that's exactly what they are.

What is a miracle? A miracle makes an opening in the wall that separates this world and another. A miracle is a wonder, a beam of God's supernatural power injected into history. A miracle is a happening that cannot be explained in terms of ordinary life.

Christ performed at least thirty-five miracles in the Bible—walking on water, healing the sick, multiplying loaves and fish, turning water into wine and even raising the dead.

Why did Christ perform so many miracles? Did He do it to demonstrate His power to the people or to solidify their faith? Did He do miracles to dramatically show that God took an interest in His creation? The answer is yes. Jesus performed miracles in order to give God glory. Perhaps the greatest miracle was the fact that Jesus—the Word—became flesh and dwelt among us. He is the visible expression of the invisible God.

God doesn't always perform miracles at our every petition, but don't underestimate His power. Next time you seek a miracle, don't forget He is not a magician—but don't be surprised if His miracle is greater than anything you could ever imagine.

**"The way may be open as never before for the gift of miracles to become more evident in our churches."
—C. Peter Wagner**

A GOD WHO WORKS MIRACLES

KEY VERSE

"At the time of sacrifice, the prophet Elijah stepped forward and prayed, 'O LORD, God of Abraham, Isaac and Israel, let it be known today that you are God in Israel and that I am your servant and have done all these things at your command. Answer me, O LORD, answer me, so these people will know that you, O LORD, are God, and that you are turning their hearts back again.'

"Then the fire of the LORD fell and burned up the sacrifice, the wood, the stones and the soil, and also licked up the water in the trench.

"When all the people saw this, they fell prostrate and cried, 'The LORD—he is God! The LORD—he is God!'" 1 Kings 18:36-39

BIBLICAL BASIS

1 Kings 17:1; 18:16-46; John 10:31,32,37,38

THE BIG IDEA

Our God is powerful and works countless miracles.

WARM UP (5-10 MINUTES)

DYNAMIC DUOS

• Divide students into pairs. Give each pair a pencil and a piece of paper.
• Have the pairs spend three minutes making a list of all of the characteristics they have in common. These characteristics might include hair color, they both have one brother, or they were born in the same city. The goal is to have students learn more about one another, thereby building a stronger sense of community in your group.
• When the pairs have finished, have them count up the number of characteristics they share. Give the pair with the most things in common the "Dynamic Duo Award" and reward them with a prize such as a large candy bar.

Fold

77

THINGS TO THINK ABOUT (OPTIONAL)

• Use the questions on page 81 after or as a part of "In the Word."
1. If God can heal any sickness, why doesn't He heal every sickness?

2. What do you do when you believe God for a miracle, but nothing seems to happen?

3. Is every act of God a miracle? Why or why not?

PARENT PAGE

• Distribute page to parents.

TEAM EFFORT—JUNIOR HIGH/MIDDLE SCHOOL (15-20 Minutes)

YOU WON'T BELIEVE WHAT GOD DID!

As we stand in a supermarket checkout line, we are surrounded by tabloid newspapers whose headlines proclaim all sorts of "miracles." These include claims of unusual births, amazing diets and even visits from extraterrestrials.

• Divide your students into groups of five students each. Give each group a large sheet of newsprint or poster board, pencils, and either felt-tip pens or crayons. Explain that each group is to design the front page of a newspaper entitled "You Won't Believe What God Did." All of their front-page headlines should come from the miracles in the Old Testament.

• You may want to give them some ideas of stories they could include as headlines. Examples include the parting of the Red Sea, Jonah swallowed by the huge fish and Joshua's capture of Jericho.

• After each group is done, ask them to present their front-page headlines to the entire group. On a chalkboard or overhead compile a list of all of the miracles mentioned.

TEAM EFFORT—HIGH SCHOOL (15-20 Minutes)

MIRACLES THEN AND NOW

• Divide students into groups of five. Give them paper and pencils and ask them to do two things:
   1. List at least two miraculous answers to prayer from the Old Testament.
   2. List at least two miraculous answers to prayer from your own life.

• After they have completed their lists, discuss the following questions:
1. Which list was easier to come up with? Why?
2. Do you think God worked more miracles in the past then He does in the present?
3. What would you say to someone who claims that God works just as many miracles today, but that we just don't always notice them?

IN THE WORD (25-30 Minutes)

THREE MAJOR MIRACLES

• Give each student a copy of "Three Major Miracles" on pages 79-80 and a pen or pencil, or display a copy using an overhead projector.

• Discuss the questions with the whole group.

There are countless examples of miracles in the Old Testament. One particular prophet, Elijah, experienced three major miracles—all in one day!

MIRACLE #1: THE RUN OF BAAL
Read I Kings 18:16-40.
1. At the beginning of the passage, what was Israel's attitude toward God?

2. How do you think the 450 prophets of Baal and 400 prophets of Asherah felt as they saw lone Elijah, the prophet of God, walking up Mount Carmel?

3. If you had been an observer of what happened in verses 25-29, how would you describe what occurred?

4. Using three words, describe Elijah's attitude in verses 36 and 37.

5. Why did Elijah order the prophets of Baal to be killed?

MIRACLE #2: THE RAIN
Read I Kings 17:1 and I Kings 18:41-45.
1. Why did God choose that particular day to bring rain to the dry land?

2. What does this passage tell you about Elijah's faith in God?

MIRACLE #3: THE RUN
Read I Kings 18:45,46.
1. What do you suppose Ahab was thinking as Elijah raced ahead of him, even though Ahab was riding a horse-drawn chariot?

2. What do these two verses tell us about God's power within us?

SO WHAT?
• Divide students into groups of three to form prayer triplets.

Often our prayers to God are requests that others could help us with. We ask for help in a test, healing for a sore ankle or just to have a good day. There's nothing wrong with involving God in every aspect of our life, no matter how small. However, God is a big God. He wants to work in big ways.
What's a big request you want to ask of God?

Take a few minutes to pray for "big things" for one another. Ask God for big miracles. Be as specific as you can in your prayer, and then wait for the next few days, weeks or months to see how God answers!

Fold

⬤N THE WORD

THREE MAJOR MIRACLES

There are countless examples of miracles in the Old Testament. One particular prophet, Elijah, experienced three major miracles—all in one day!

Miracle #1: The Ruin of Baal
Read 1 Kings 18:16-40.

1. At the beginning of the passage, what was Israel's attitude toward God?

2. How do you think the 450 prophets of Baal and 400 prophets of Asherah felt as they saw lone Elijah, the prophet of God, walking up Mount Carmel?

3. If you had been an observer of what happened in verses 25-29, how would you describe what occurred?

4. Using three words, describe Elijah's attitude in verses 36 and 37.

5. Why did Elijah order the prophets of Baal to be killed?

Miracle #2: The Rain
Read 1 Kings 17:1 and 1 Kings 18:41-44.

1. Why did God choose that particular day to bring rain to the dry land?

2. What does this passage tell you about Elijah's faith in God?

....

....

Miracle #3: The Run
Read 1 Kings 18:45,46.

1. What do you suppose Ahab was thinking as Elijah raced ahead of him, even though Ahab was riding a horse-drawn chariot?

....

....

2. What do these two verses tell us about God's power within us?

....

....

So What?

Often our prayers to God are requests that our neighbors could help us with. We ask for help in a test, healing for a sore ankle, or just to have a good day. There's nothing wrong with involving God in every aspect of our life, no matter how small. However, God is a big God. He wants to work in big ways.

What's a big request you want to ask of God?

....

....

Take a few minutes to pray for "big things" for one another. Ask God for big miracles. Be as specific as you can in your prayer, and then wait for the next few days, weeks or months to see how God answers!

THINGS TO THINK ABOUT

1. If God can heal any sickness, why doesn't He heal every sickness?

....
....
....

2. What do you do when you believe God for a miracle, but nothing seems to happen?

....
....
....

3. Is every act of God a miracle? Why or why not?

....
....
....

A GOD WHO WORKS MIRACLES

ᴘarent ᴘage

Believe It or Not

The Old Testament is exploding with examples of God's miracles. Often these miracles followed persistent prayer on the part of His people.

As a family, read 1 Kings 17:17-24 out loud.

1. Why do you think God did the miracle of healing the woman's son?

....

....

....

2. How did the woman respond to God's miracle?

....

....

The same God is working today. He wants to work miracles in our own lives. Our part is to seek Him through prayer.

Have each family member answer the following two questions:

1. What miracle would I like to see God do in my own life?

....

....

....

2. What miracle would I like to see God do in our family?

....

....

Write down the answers to these questions. For the next two weeks, post these requests on your refrigerator, bathroom mirrors, in your cars—wherever they will jog your memory. Give each family member a copy of these prayer requests. At the end of two weeks, come together and discuss the ways family members have seen God answer these prayers.

Session 7 "A God Who Works Miracles"
Date ....

A GOD WHO FORGIVES

KEY VERSE

"Then David said to Nathan, 'I have sinned against the LORD.'

"Nathan replied, 'The LORD has taken away your sin. You are not going to die. But because by doing this you have made the enemies of the LORD show utter contempt, the son born to you will die.'" 2 Samuel 12:13,14

BIBLICAL BASIS

2 Samuel 11—12;
Mark 2:13,14;
Luke 15:11-32;
John 8:2-11;
Acts 9:1-19;
Romans 3:23;
1 John 1:9

THE BIG IDEA

No matter what sin you have committed, God does forgive you. However, you still may face tough consequences.

AIMS OF THIS SESSION

During this session you will guide students to:
• Examine the story of David and the terrible sin he committed;
• Discover the same forgiving God that David did;
• Implement how to ask God for forgiveness for a sin they have recently committed.

WARM UP

ALPHABET PRAISE—

An activity to help students focus on God's amazing characteristics.

TEAM EFFORT— JUNIOR HIGH/ MIDDLE SCHOOL

GETTING CAUGHT—

A probing discussion into typical responses when caught doing something wrong.

TEAM EFFORT— HIGH SCHOOL

THE TRUTH IS OUT!—

A true example revealing the pervasiveness of human guilt and sin.

IN THE WORD

THERE'S BAD NEWS AND THERE'S GOOD NEWS—

A Bible study exposing both David's sin and God's forgiveness.

THINGS TO THINK ABOUT (OPTIONAL)

Questions to get students thinking and talking on a deeper level about God's forgiveness.

PARENT PAGE

A tool to get the session into the home and allow parents and young people to ask for forgiveness from one another.

**A GOD
WHO FORGIVES**

LEADER'S DEVOTIONAL

"If we confess our sins, he is faithful and just and will forgive us our sins and purify us from all unrighteousness" (1 John 1:9).

At a conference for the United States governors several years ago, an interesting question was raised during one of the political debates: "What is the greatest thing in the world?" It was absolutely quiet. None of the governors had an answer. Finally a young aide took the microphone and said, "The greatest thing in the world is that we can walk away from yesterday."

I'm not even sure if that young aide knew that she had just summarized the essence of the gospel of Jesus Christ. The good news of the Christian faith is that we can walk away from yesterday. The apostle Paul could walk away from his persecution of the Christians and answer the call to Christ (see Acts 9:1-19). The woman taken in adultery could walk away from her destructive lifestyle into a new life with Jesus Christ (see John 8:2-11). Matthew could walk away from his job as a crooked tax collector and follow Christ into a new life (see Mark 2:13,14). The prodigal son could walk away from his life of moral failure in the far country and walk into the loving, forgiving arms of his father (see Luke 15:11-32).

To be able to walk away from the failures and guilt of yesterday lies at the very heart of forgiveness. This is no call to cop out, drop out or otherwise escape responsibility, but it is a liberating message that no one—absolutely no one—is tied to a past from which there is no release. The gospel gladly sings of the possibility of new beginnings. Aren't you glad you are a Christian?

**"When it comes to confessed sins, our Lord is absent-minded."
—Peter Gilchrist**

A GOD WHO FORGIVES

KEY **V**ERSE

"Then David said to Nathan, 'I have sinned against the LORD.' Nathan replied, 'The LORD has taken away your sin. You are not going to die. But because by doing this you have made the enemies of the Lord show utter contempt, the son born to you will die.'" 2 Samuel 12:13,14

BIBLICAL **B**ASIS

2 Samuel 11—12; Mark 2:13,14; Luke 15:11-32; John 8:2-11; Acts 9:1-19; Romans 3:23; 1 John 1:9

THE **B**IG **I**DEA

No matter what sin you have committed, God does forgive you. However, you still may face tough consequences.

WARM **U**P (5-10 MINUTES)

ALPHABET PRAISE

• To get students thinking about God's characteristics, explain that you need their help. Divide your students into groups of four and give each group paper and a pen or pencil. Ask them to make an "Alphabet Praise List" in which they make a list of one characteristic of God for each letter of the alphabet. For example, the list may begin: Awesome, Beautiful, Courageous, Daring, Excellent.

• Once each group is done with their lists, have one spokesperson from each group read the group's list. This will have the most impact in the group if all other students remain quiet and if the lists are read with no discussion between each list.

So What?

1. What do you need to ask forgiveness from God for right now?
....

2. Are there any consequences you may still have to face for what you have done?
....

3. What steps do you need to take to make it right?
....

4. How can you show forgiveness to others this week?
....

THINGS TO **T**HINK **A**BOUT (OPTIONAL)

• Use the questions on page 92 after or as a part of "In the Word."

1. Are there any people God won't forgive? Explain your answer.
....

2. Are there any sins God won't forgive? Why or why not?
....

3. **Does God also forget our sins when He forgives us? Explain.**
....

PARENT **P**AGE

• Distribute page to parents.

Fold

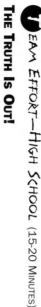

GETTING CAUGHT

• Read the following story to the whole group.
• Discuss the questions together.
• Option: Students could remain in their "Warm Up" groups of four. Give each group a copy of "Getting Caught" on page 87 and have them read and discuss the story.

Volleyball tryouts are quickly approaching. You and your friend decide to practice volleyball after school at your house. It's so hot outside that you both decide to practice inside your living room. There's plenty of room and it's air-conditioned.

Your little sister warns you, "You're not supposed to play ball in the house."
"No big deal," you reply, "we'll be careful."
Just as you finish this sentence, there's a loud CRASH! Peering down at the floor, you see the shattered remnants of what had been an expensive mirror near your front door.
A few seconds later, your mom runs into the room and asks, "What happened? How did the mirror get broken?"
You've been caught!

1. How do you respond?

    Ask innocently, "What glass on the floor?"
    Argue, "I never liked that mirror anyway."
    Tell her that your friend did it.
    Admit what happened, but be defensive about it.
    Admit what happened and ask for forgiveness.
    Admit what happened, ask for forgiveness and offer to pay for a new mirror.

2. Why is our first reaction so often to blame others for our mistakes?

3. Why do we hate to get caught?

THE TRUTH IS OUT!

• Read the following story to the whole group.
• Discuss the questions together.
• Option: Students could remain in their "Warm Up" groups of four. Give them a copy of "The Truth Is Out" on page 88 and have them read and discuss the story.

One day, the well-known author and creator of detective Sherlock Holmes, Sir Arthur Conan Doyle, decided to play a practical joke on his ten closest friends. He sent each of them a telegram with the following message: "The truth is out. Flee immediately."

All ten did just that! They left town!
Doyle never would have guessed that his friends would have been so ashamed of something they had done.

Read Romans 3:23.
1. How does this story confirm Romans 3:23?

2. Do you agree or disagree that most people would flee if they received such a message? Why or why not?

3. What should a person who feels guilty do?

IN THE WORD (25-30 MINUTES)

THERE'S BAD NEWS AND THERE'S GOOD NEWS!

• Divide students into groups of three or four.
• Give each student a copy of "There's Bad News and There's Good News!" on pages 89-91 and a pen or pencil or display a copy using an overhead projector.
• Have students complete the study.

David, a leader anointed by the Lord, experienced many personal and spiritual triumphs. However, he was human. He made mistakes. One particular sin of David's is recorded in 2 Samuel 11-12.

THE BAD NEWS
Read 2 Samuel 11:1-5.
1. At what point did David's sin begin?

2. Who else besides David committed sin?

Not only did David commit adultery, but he tried to cover up his sin. Read 2 Samuel 11:6-13 to see how David tried to deceive Uriah the Hittite.
3. What do we learn from these verses about Uriah?

4. How do you think David was feeling after Uriah refused to sleep with his wife?

5. What is David's state of mind in 2 Samuel 11:14-17?

THE GOOD NEWS
To see how God got David's attention about his sin, read 2 Samuel 12:1-10.
1. What was Nathan's clever way of convincing David of his sin?

2. God used Nathan to get David's attention. How else do you think God could have gotten David's attention?

3. Read 2 Samuel 12:13-23. What were the consequences David still had to face, even though he repented?

4. Why do you think God didn't simply heal David and Bathsheba's son?

5. Why did David's attitude change once his son was dead?

Fold

*T*EAM *E*FFORT

GETTING CAUGHT

Volleyball tryouts are quickly approaching. You and your friend decide to practice volleyball after school at your house. It's so hot outside that you both decide to practice inside your living room. There's plenty of room and it's air conditioned.

Your little sister warns you, "You're not supposed to play ball in the house."

"No big deal," you reply, "we'll be careful."

Just as you finish this sentence, there is a loud CRASH! Peering down at the floor, you see the shattered remnants of what had been an expensive mirror near your front door.

A few seconds later, your mom runs into the room and asks, "What happened? How did the mirror get broken?" You've been caught.

1. How do you respond?

....
....
....

Ask innocently, "What glass on the floor?"

Argue, "I never liked that mirror anyway."

Tell her that your friend did it.

Admit what happened, but be defensive about it.

Admit what happened and ask for forgiveness.

Admit what happened, ask for forgiveness and offer to pay for a new mirror.

2. Why is our first reaction so often to blame others for our mistakes?

....
....
....

3. Why do we hate to get caught?

....
....
....

A GOD
WHO FORGIVES

TEAM EFFORT

THE TRUTH IS OUT!

One day, the well-known author and creator of the detective Sherlock Holmes, Sir Arthur Conan Doyle, decided to play a practical joke on his ten closest friends. He sent each of them a telegram with the following message: "The truth is out. Flee immediately."

All ten did just that! They left town!

Doyle never would have guessed that his friends would have been so ashamed of something they had done.

Read Romans 3:23.

1. How does this story confirm Romans 3:23?

2. Do you agree or disagree that most people would flee if they received such a message? Why or why not?

3. What should a person who feels guilty do?

IN THE WORD

THERE'S BAD NEWS AND THERE'S GOOD NEWS!

David, a leader anointed by the Lord, experienced many personal and spiritual triumphs. However, he was human. He made mistakes. He committed sins. One particular sin of David is recorded in 2 Samuel 11—12.

The Bad News

Read 2 Samuel 11:1-5.

1. At what point did David's sin begin?

2. Who else besides David committed sin?

Not only did David commit adultery, but he tried to cover up his sin. Read 2 Samuel 11:6-13 to see how David tried to deceive Uriah the Hittite.

3. What do we learn from these verses about Uriah?

4. How do you think David was feeling after Uriah refused to sleep with his wife?

5. What is David's state of mind in 2 Samuel 11:14-17?

A GOD
WHO FORGIVES

The Good News

To see how God got David's attention about his sin, read 2 Samuel 12:1-10.

1. What was Nathan's clever way of convincing David of his sin?

_____

_____

2. God used Nathan to get David's attention. How else do you think God could have gotten David's attention?

_____

_____

3. Read 2 Samuel 12:13-23. What were the consequences David still had to face, even after he repented?

_____

_____

4. Why do you think God didn't simply heal David and Bathsheba's son?

_____

_____

5. Why did David's attitude change once his son was dead?

_____

_____

So What?

1. What do you need to ask forgiveness from God for right now?

_____

_____

2. Are there any consequences you may still have to face for what you have done?

_____

_____

3. What steps do you need to take to make it right?

....
....
....

4. How can you show forgiveness to others this week?

....
....
....

A GOD
WHO FORGIVES

THINGS TO THINK ABOUT

1. Are there any people God won't forgive? Explain your answer.

....
....
....

2. Are there any sins God won't forgive? Why or why not?

....
....
....

3. Does God also forget our sins when He forgives us? Explain.

....
....
....

A GOD
WHO FORGIVES

PARENT PAGE

DON'T LET ANOTHER DAY GO BY

As a family, read 2 Samuel 11:1-17 and 2 Samuel 12:1-14 together. After David committed adultery with Bathsheba in 2 Samuel 11, he asked God for forgiveness. God granted him forgiveness and continued to use David in mighty ways. David's story shows us the power of forgiveness to bring freedom and joy back into a person's life.

As family members, at times you undoubtedly rub each other the wrong way, hurt each other's feelings and ignore each other's needs. After all, no person or family is perfect!

1. How would your family be different if you repeatedly confessed and forgave each other?

2. How can your family practice forgiving each other in the future?

Take some time right now to search your heart. Ask yourself the following questions:

3. How have I sinned against a family member recently?

4. Have I asked forgiveness from that person yet?

If not, don't let another day go by. There's no better time than right now. Go to that family member, confess your sin and ask for his or her forgiveness. If you're not sure how to do it, try beginning your conversation by saying, "I need to ask your forgiveness for..."

Session 8 "A God Who Forgives"
Date

ORDINARY PEOPLE WITH EXTRAORDINARY QUALITIES

LEADER'S PEP TALK

I wanted to be Wonder Woman. My younger brother, Matt, wanted to be Superman. We used to wake up at the crack of dawn every Saturday morning, run downstairs, turn on the television set and watch our favorite heroes, Wonder Woman and Superman, fight for truth, justice and the American way.

Finding a hero these days is not so easy. Students feel distant from their teachers and school administrators, abandoned by their parents and disillusioned by popular athletes and entertainers.

Maybe it's time to look in a new direction for our heroes. Maybe it's time we as youth workers point students to the pages of the Old Testament and the men and women whose lives give those pages flavor as their new heroes.

The cool thing about the heroes of the Old Testament is that they are regular people. As I read about them, I have yet to discover any individual who had superhuman powers on his or her own, or who was always perfect, or who acted like a super saint all of the time. Instead, I see sinners in relationship with God the Father. I see normal ordinary people with some extraordinary qualities. This is true heroism: Taking what God has given you and doing your best to glorify Him with it.

As your students study this unit, hopefully they will also realize that they too can be ordinary people with extraordinary qualities. They too can try their best to love their Lord with all their heart, mind and soul, and to make His love known to others. May these heroes from the past inspire your students to become godly heroes in the present and future.

SAMUEL:
LIVING WITH YOUR EARS OPEN

KEY VERSE

"The LORD came and stood there, calling as at the other times, 'Samuel! Samuel!' Then Samuel said, 'Speak, for your servant is listening.'" 1 Samuel 3:10

BIBLICAL BASIS

1 Samuel 2:29; 3:1-20; 8:6-10; Jeremiah 33:3; Romans 8:35-37

THE BIG IDEA

The best way to hear the Lord's voice is to listen for Him.

AIMS OF THIS SESSION

During this session you will guide students to:

• Examine the model of Samuel, a teenager who heard from God;

• Discover their need to listen attentively for the Lord;

• Implement a time to listen for the Lord.

WARM UP

IT WAS THE BEST OF TIMES AND THE WORST OF TIMES—

Students describe what has happened to them in the past week.

TEAM EFFORT— JUNIOR HIGH/ MIDDLE SCHOOL

WHO'S TALKING NOW?—

Students try to discern each others' voices.

TEAM EFFORT— HIGH SCHOOL

ARE YOUR EARS OPEN?—

A real-life example of a young person living with his ears open.

IN THE WORD

WHAT WAS THE DIFFERENCE?—

A Bible study that compares the listening abilities of Eli and young Samuel.

THINGS TO THINK ABOUT (OPTIONAL)

Questions to get students thinking and talking about the difficulties of sharing what we hear from the Lord with others.

PARENT PAGE

A tool to get the session into the home and allow parents and young people to talk over the importance of listening to the Lord and receiving confirmation from Scripture.

SAMUEL:
LIVING WITH YOUR
EARS OPEN

LEADER'S DEVOTIONAL

"Who shall separate us from the love of Christ? Shall trouble or hardship or persecution or famine or nakedness or danger or sword? As it is written: 'For your sake we face death all day long; we are considered as sheep to be slaughtered.' No, in all these things we are more than conquerors through him who loved us" (Romans 8:35-37).

For a Christian youth speaker, it had been one of those crummy days. I walked down from the platform of a high school auditorium, feeling depressed and dejected. I hadn't connected with the audience. Basically, what I thought would work at the assembly fell flat. I mumbled an apology to the principal and walked to my car, feeling broken and downcast. The entire day, I let this bomb of an assembly get to me.

That night my sleep was interrupted by a dream—I believe God gave me this dream. I found myself in the same auditorium as I was earlier in the day. It was empty except for one person sitting in the front row—Jesus. As I walked to the platform, Jesus rose to His feet and gave me a standing ovation! He cheered, He whistled, He applauded with enthusiasm before I even spoke.

When I awoke, I remember smiling so big, my face hurt. God loves me not for what I do but for who I am—His child.

What about you? Do you know that Jesus daily gives you a standing ovation? He loved you enough to die for you. I have this feeling if He carried a wallet in heaven, your picture and mine are in that wallet. Isn't it nice to be loved?

**"Listening is the language of love."
—Ned Brines**

SAMUEL:
LIVING WITH YOUR EARS OPEN

KEY VERSE

"The LORD came and stood there, calling as at the other times, 'Samuel! Samuel!' Then Samuel said, 'Speak, for your servant is listening.'" 1 Samuel 3:10

BIBLICAL BASIS

1 Samuel 2:29; 3:1-20; 8:6-10; Jeremiah 33:3; Romans 8:35-37

THE BIG IDEA

The best way to hear the Lord's voice is to listen for Him.

WARM UP (5-10 MINUTES)

IT WAS THE BEST OF TIMES AND THE WORST OF TIMES

• Divide the students into groups of three or four.
• Give each group a copy of "It Was the Best of Times and the Worst of Times" on page 99, or display a copy using an overhead projector.
• Have the groups discuss the following questions:
1. What is the best thing that has happened to you this week?

2. What is the worst thing that has happened to you this week?

3. Describe the last time you were talking with someone and you didn't think they were listening to you. How did you feel?

Fold

Let's practice...

• Have students turn over this sheet of paper or give them each a piece of paper. Have them write "Speak, for your servant is listening" (1 Samuel 3:10) at the top. Give them three to five minutes to pray individually about a specific situation they are facing this week. Instruct them to spend at least half of the time trying to listen to God's plan for them. Have them write down what they think God is saying to them.

• You might want to play worship music in the background to minimize distractions. Or, you could take your students to a quiet place outdoors to reduce the potential distractions in your classroom.

On the back of this sheet of paper (or the sheet of paper your leader gives you), write "Speak, for your servant is listening" (1 Samuel 3:10). Then spend a few minutes praying about a specific situation that you are facing this week. Spend at least half the time trying to listen to God's plan for you. Write down anything you think God is saying to you.

THINGS TO THINK ABOUT (OPTIONAL)

• Use the questions on page 103 after or as a part of "In the Word."
1. Why didn't Samuel want to tell Eli what God had revealed to Him?

2. Why do you think Eli responded the way he did in 1 Samuel 3:18?

3. In what situations do you think it would be the toughest to share with others what you feel God is leading you to do?

PARENT PAGE

• Distribute page to parents.

Who's Talking Now?

- Have all your students spread out around the room as far as possible from each other and then close their eyes. Slowly walk around the room. Explain that whenever you tap a student on his or her shoulder, that person must ask "Who's talking now?" The other students, with their eyes still closed, try to guess which student is talking.
- Do this about seven to ten times, selecting a different student each time to ask "Who's talking now?"
- Discuss the following questions:

1. How were you able to tell who was talking?

....

2. Which voices were easiest to recognize? Why?

....

TEAM EFFORT—HIGH SCHOOL (15-20 MINUTES)

ARE YOUR EARS OPEN?

- Keeping the same groups from the "Warm Up," give each group a copy of "Are Your Ears Open?" on page 100 or display a copy using an overhead projector.
- Have the groups read and discuss the story.

A twenty-year-old named Loren Cunningham was part of a gospel singing quartet that was traveling to the Bahamas. One night after ministering, Loren laid down on his bed and opened his Bible, asking God to speak into his mind. Suddenly, he envisioned a map of the world. Only the map was alive, moving! He could see all the continents, with waves from the ocean washing onto their shores.

The ocean waves became waves of young people—teenagers—covering the continents. They were caring for people on street corners and outside bars. They were preaching from house to house. They were praying with strangers.

Loren wondered, "Was that really You, Lord?" Loren prayed, "God, is this vision from You? Is my future somehow linked to waves of young people?" God seemed to confirm that it was His vision.

Young people going out as missionaries—what an amazing vision! Since then, Loren has founded an organization known as YWAM—Youth With A Mission. In the thirty years since his vision, hundreds of thousands of young "YWAMers" have swept into every continent to share the gospel.

1. Would you conclude that Loren heard from God?

....

2. What kind of a person do you think Loren was?

....

3. Have you ever felt as if you heard from the Lord? If so, what happened?

....

4. How do we hear God?

....

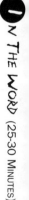

IN THE WORD (25-30 MINUTES)

WHAT WAS THE DIFFERENCE?

- Give each student a copy of "What Was the Difference?" on pages 101-102 and a pen or pencil.
- Discuss the following study with the whole group.

Notice that Eli, the priest of Shiloh, had difficulties hearing God's voice while Samuel, a young teenager, was available to hear from God. Let's explore the difference between Eli and Samuel.

ELI

1. Read 1 Samuel 2:29. What sins did the Lord see in Eli?

....

2. What were Eli's priorities?

....

3. How did Eli's wrong priorities muffle his ability to listen for the Lord's voice?

....

SAMUEL

Now let's look at how Samuel shows two important qualities in a person who is able to listen to the Lord. Read 1 Samuel 3:1-20.

Samuel desired to be close to God.

1. Where did Samuel sleep?

....

2. How does the place where Samuel slept reflect his desire to be close to God?

....

3. Can someone who is far from God hear His voice? Why or why not?

....

Samuel desired to serve God.

1. How is Samuel's response to Eli in 1 Samuel 3:5,6,8 similar to his response to God in 1 Samuel 8:10?

....

2. Why do you think Samuel refers to himself as God's "servant"?

....

3. How is a servant attitude important in listening to God's voice?

....

SO WHAT?

The Master Architect

We often act as if we are the architects of our own lives. We design our own plans for our lives, and maybe ask God to bless what we have already designed.

How far this is from the truth! God is the Master Architect. Our job is to follow His plans, not try to create our own.

1. What are the problems with designing your own blueprint?

....

2. What keeps you from letting God, the Master Architect, give you His blueprint for your life?

....

3. How can you get this week's blueprint from the Master Architect?

....

SAMUEL:
LIVING WITH YOUR
EARS OPEN

WARM UP

IT WAS THE BEST OF TIMES AND THE WORST OF TIMES

1. What is the best thing that has happened to you this week?

_____

_____

_____

2. What is the worst thing that has happened to you this week?

_____

_____

_____

3. Describe the last time you were talking with someone and you didn't think they were listening to you. How did you feel?

_____

_____

_____

**SAMUEL:
LIVING WITH YOUR
EARS OPEN**

*T*EAM *E*FFORT

ARE YOUR EARS OPEN?

A twenty-year-old named Loren Cunningham was part of a gospel singing quartet that was traveling to the Bahamas. One night after ministering, Loren laid down on his bed and opened his Bible, asking God to speak into his mind.

Suddenly, he envisioned a map of the world. Only the map was alive, moving! He could see all the continents, with waves from the ocean crashing onto their shores.

The ocean waves became waves of young people—teenagers—covering the continents. They were preaching from house to house. They were praying with strangers. They were caring for people on street corners and outside bars.

Loren wondered, "Was that really You, Lord?"

Loren prayed, "God, is this vision from You? Is my future somehow linked to waves of young people?" God seemed to confirm that it was His vision.

Young people going out as missionaries—what an amazing vision! Since then, Loren has founded an organization known as YWAM—Youth With A Mission. In the thirty years since his vision, hundreds of thousands of young "YWAMers" have swept into every continent to share the gospel. [1]

I. Would you conclude that Loren heard from God?

....

....

....

2. What kind of a person do you think Loren was?

....

....

....

3. Have you ever felt as if you heard from the Lord? If so, what happened?

....

....

....

4. How do we hear God?

....

....

....

1. Adapted from Loren Cunningham with Janice Rogers, *Is That Really You, God?* (Old Tappan, N.J.: Chosen Books, 1984), pp. 29-30.

SAMUEL:
LIVING WITH YOUR
EARS OPEN

● IN THE WORD

WHAT WAS THE DIFFERENCE?

Notice that Eli, the priest of Shiloh, had difficulties hearing God's voice while Samuel, a young teenager, was available to hear from God. Let's explore the difference between Eli and Samuel.

Eli

1. Read 1 Samuel 2:29. What sins did the Lord see in Eli?

....

....

2. What were Eli's priorities?

....

....

3. How did Eli's wrong priorities muffle his ability to listen for the Lord's voice?

....

....

Samuel

Now let's look at Samuel, who shows two important qualities in a person who is able to listen to the Lord. Read 1 Samuel 3:1-20.
Samuel desired to be close to God.

1. Where did Samuel sleep?

....

....

2. How does the place where Samuel slept reflect his desire to be close to God?

....

....

3. Can someone who is far from God hear His voice? Why or why not?

....

....

**SAMUEL:
LIVING WITH YOUR
EARS OPEN**

Samuel desired to serve God.

1. How is Samuel's response to Eli in 1 Samuel 3:5, 6 and 8 similar to his response to God in 1 Samuel 8:10?

    ....

    ....

2. Why do you think Samuel refers to himself as God's "servant"?

    ....

    ....

3. How is a servant attitude important in listening to God's voice?

    ....

    ....

So What?

The Master Architect

We often act as if we are the architects of our own lives. We design our own plans for our lives, and maybe ask God to bless what we have already designed.

How far this is from the truth! God is the Master Architect. Our job is to follow His plans, not try to create our own.

1. What are the problems with designing your own blueprint?

    ....

    ....

2. What keeps you from letting God, the Master Architect, give you His blueprint for your life?

    ....

    ....

3. How can you get this week's blueprint from the Master Architect?

    ....

    ....

Let's practice...

On the back of this sheet of paper (or a sheet of paper your leader gives you), write "Speak, for your servant is listening" (1 Samuel 3:10). Then spend a few minutes praying about a specific situation that you are facing this week. Spend at least half the time trying to listen to God's plan for you. Write down anything you think God is saying to you.

SAMUEL:
LIVING WITH YOUR
EARS OPEN

*T*HINGS TO THINK ABOUT

1. Why didn't Samuel want to tell Eli what God had revealed to Him?

....

....

....

2. Why do you think Eli responded the way he did in 1 Samuel 3:18?

....

....

....

3. In what situations do you think it would be the toughest to share with others what you feel God is leading you to do?

....

....

....

SAMUEL:
LIVING WITH YOUR
EARS OPEN

ᴘARENT ᴘAGE

LISTEN CLOSELY NOW

Martin Luther once taught "Prayer changes from talking into being silent. And then our being silent can change into listening to God."

This is similar to the words of Jeremiah 33:3, "'Call to me and I will answer you and tell you great and mighty things you did not know.'"

1. What does Jeremiah 33:3 tell you about the balance between talking and listening to God?

_____

_____

_____

2. What benefits do we receive as we listen to God?

_____

_____

Dan, a high school sophomore, had been going to the same church with his parents for ten years. However, he had only gotten serious about his relationship with Christ a few months ago. Last night at dinner, Dan's parents told him that due to the major fights they had been having lately, they felt that God wanted them to file for divorce.

1. Do you think Dan's parents truly heard God's voice? Explain your answer.

_____

_____

_____

2. God's voice in the present will never contradict His voice in the past, namely Scripture. Besides checking what we think God is saying to us in His Word, how else can we confirm whether what we are hearing is actually God's voice?

_____

_____

_____

3. If you wanted confirmation from two or three other Christians you respect, who would you go to?

_____

_____

_____

Session 9 "Samuel: Living with Your Ears Open" Date _____

ESTHER:
FOR SUCH A TIME AS THIS

KEY VERSE

"For if you remain silent at this time, relief and deliverance for the Jews will arise from another place, but you and your father's family will perish. And who knows but that you have come to royal position for such a time as this?" Esther 4:14

BIBLICAL BASIS

Esther 1—8;
2 Timothy 2:2

THE BIG IDEA

God can use us in our unique circumstances to help others know Him.

AIMS OF THIS SESSION

During this session you will guide students to:
- Examine how God is working in their lives at this particular time;
- Discover the value of risking all for God, even if the losses could be great;
- Implement a specific way to use their unique circumstances to help others know Him.

WARM UP

IN THIS ROOM...—
Students share what is unique about their circumstances, characteristics and backgrounds.

TEAM EFFORT— JUNIOR HIGH/ MIDDLE SCHOOL

MY FAVORITE JOB—
Students examine how God can use their job situations to draw people close to Him.

TEAM EFFORT— HIGH SCHOOL

IF I WERE...—
Students brainstorm how various types of jobs can be used by God.

IN THE WORD

A CLOSE LOOK AT THE KEY PLAYERS—
A Bible study that takes a deeper look at the main characters in the story of Esther.

THINGS TO THINK ABOUT (OPTIONAL)

Questions to get students thinking and talking about obeying God.

PARENT PAGE

A tool to get the session into the home and allow parents and young people to think about the right timing and the right choices in their families.

ESTHER: FOR SUCH A TIME AS THIS

LEADER'S DEVOTIONAL

"And the things you have heard me say in the presence of many witnesses entrust to reliable [people] who will also be qualified to teach others" (2 Timothy 2:2).

A judge in a juvenile court was battling a massive crime wave. Kid after kid was hauled before him mainly from the same neighborhood. Finally the judge, totally exasperated, questioned the next defendant: "Where did you learn this stuff?" The adolescent replied, "Rocko taught me." When the next case came up, the judge repeated the question: "Who taught you to steal?" The answer was the same: "Rocko did."

Over the next week the judge found 33 juvenile delinquents who had picked up their criminal skills from this now notorious Rocko character. Realizing that Rocko was quite possibly the person who was key to cutting the crime rate in this neighborhood, the judge instructed the district attorney to bring Rocko to him.

Two days later Rocko stood before the bench. "Well, what do you have to say for yourself?" the judge demanded. "I've got a jail full of minors whose lives you've corrupted. How could you do such a thing?"

"Eddie taught me," the young man replied.

There's a lesson here for those of us who work with kids. Ordinary people can influence others—for good or for bad. God uses ordinary people to influence young people through personal relationships. God uses any circumstance or relationship to get a person's attention.

Imagine the movement that began with a handful of weak-kneed people in an upstairs room in Jerusalem. By the end of the first century, this small group had turned the world upside down. And today you and I are a part of that same movement! Who knows, one day another Christian prophetic voice will lead the nation and someone will ask, "Where did you get your start?" The reply will be: "My youth worker taught me."

**"You are the only Jesus somebody knows."
—A missionary from Africa**

ESTHER:
FOR SUCH A TIME AS THIS

K EY VERSE

"For if you remain silent at this time, relief and deliverance for the Jews will arise from another place, but you and your father's family will perish. And who knows but that you have come to royal position for such a time as this?" Esther 4:14

B IBLICAL BASIS

Esther 1—8; 2 Timothy 2:2

T HE BIG IDEA

God can use us in our unique circumstances to help others know Him.

W ARM UP (5-10 MINUTES)

IN THIS ROOM...

• Divide students into pairs. The goal of this exercise is to help students identify their unique circumstances, characteristics and situations.

• Give each of them sixty seconds to describe for their partners what is unique about themselves compared to other people in the room. In other words, what about them makes them one-of-a-kind compared to everyone else. Answers may include their parents, schools, hairstyles, clothing, backgrounds, interests, etc.

• If there is enough time, ask students to share one unique thing they learned about their partners.

―――― Fold ――――

U HINGS TO THINK ABOUT (OPTIONAL)

• Use the questions on page 115 after or as a part of "In the Word."

1. What prevents us from obeying God when He calls us to do certain things at certain times?

....

2. What might be some of the consequences for others if we refuse to obey God?

....

3. What might be some of the consequences in our own lives if we refuse to obey God's call?

....

P ARENT PAGE

• Distribute page to parents.

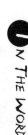

TEAM EFFORT—JUNIOR HIGH/MIDDLE SCHOOL (15-20 MINUTES)

MY FAVORITE JOB

- Have each pair join another pair to form a group of four.
- Give each student a copy of "My Favorite Job" on page 109, or display a copy using an overhead projector.
- Have groups discuss their answers to the following questions:

1. If you could have any job you wanted, what would it be?

....

2. What would be the best part of this job?

....

3. How could you help others know about the Lord through this job?

....

4. Many people believe any job can turn into full-time ministry as God uses a person to reach out to others. The key is not the job itself, but the person's attitude. Is this belief true or false? Why or why not?

....

TEAM EFFORT—HIGH SCHOOL (15-20 MINUTES)

IF I WERE...

- Have each pair join another pair to form a group of four.
- Give each student a copy of "If I Were..." on page 110 and a pen or pencil.
- Give students about three to five minutes to write down their answers.
- Have groups discuss their responses to the following:

If I were...

I could help others know about God by...

An artist

An Olympic athlete

An attorney

A fast-food worker

A state senator

A secretary

A teacher

A parent

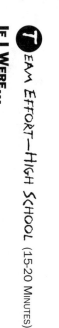

IN THE WORD (25-30 MINUTES)

A CLOSE LOOK AT THE KEY PLAYERS

- Before reading the melodrama, assign students to act out the actions, thoughts and lines of the listed biblical characters as you or a student volunteer reads the story.
- If possible, give the actors a chance to read the story to themselves before they act it out.
- Ask the rest of the students to serve as the audience to cheer on the "actors."
- After the performance, give the students copies of the questions on pages 113-114 and discuss.

Fold

---

1. How do you think God worked through Xerxes' seemingly unfair dismissal of Queen Vashti, his first wife?

....

2. Read Esther 5:9-14. How would you describe Haman?

If you were king, would you want him as your close advisor? What was he really interested in?

....

3. How was Esther treated as the queen (see Esther 4:11,15,16)?

How could this change if the king was displeased with her request to save the Jews?

....

4. How do you think Esther felt when Mordecai insisted that she conceal her Jewish identity?

....

5. What did Mordecai mean in Esther 4:14 when he warned Esther "For if you remain silent at this time, relief and deliverance for the Jews will arise from another place, but you and your father's family will perish. And who knows but that you have come to royal position for such a time as this?" (Italics added for emphasis.)

How does Esther's reply to Mordecai in verse 16 point out the serious danger she would be in?

....

SO WHAT?

1. How is God calling you to act "for such a time as this" to tell others about Him this week in...

Your home?

....

Your friendships?

....

Your school?

....

2. What might you lose if you tell others about Him?

....

3. Knowing what you might lose, why should you speak up?

....

ESTHER: FOR SUCH A TIME AS THIS

*T*EAM *EFFORT*

MY FAVORITE JOB

1. If you could have any job you wanted, what would it be?

....

....

....

2. What would be the best part of this job?

....

....

....

3. How could you help others know about the Lord through this job?

....

....

....

4. Many people believe any job can turn into full-time ministry as God uses the person to reach out to others. The key is not the job itself, but the person's attitude. Is this belief true or false? Why or why not?

....

....

....

ESTHER: FOR SUCH A TIME AS THIS

TEAM EFFORT

IF I WERE...

If I were...	I could help others know about God by...
An artist	
An Olympic athlete	
An attorney	
A fast-food worker	
A state senator	
A secretary	
A teacher	
A parent	

IN THE WORD

The Esther Melodrama

Cast:

> Narrator
>
> King Xerxes (Pronounced Zerk-zeez)
>
> Vashti (Vash-tee)
>
> Mordecai (More-duh-ki)
>
> Esther (Es-ter)
>
> Bigthana (Big-thah-nuh)
>
> Teresh (Tear-esh)
>
> Haman (Hay-mun)
>
> A guard

There once was a king of Persia named Xerxes. Xerxes was a proud and noble king. One day, he was having a wild party. Wanting to impress his friends, he called for his beautiful wife Vashti, "Vashti, come here darling." Vashti was insulted. She sighed loudly and refused to come.

Xerxes was hopping mad (Yes, he actually began to hop). He said angrily, "Vashti, I will not think of you as my wife anymore. I need a new wife."

The king sent out messengers to bring many beautiful women to the palace. When Mordecai heard that Xerxes wanted a new wife, he knew that his cousin Esther was lovely and told her "Esther, skip along to the palace." Sure enough, the king took one look at Esther and fell head over heels in love (Yes, he actually did somersaults). He asked her to marry him and she became his queen.

One problem: Mordecai had warned Esther not to tell King Xerxes that she was Jewish.

A little while later, two of the king's officers, Bigthana and Teresh, crouched nearby and dreamed up ways to kill Xerxes. Mordecai overheard their plans. He said, "Hark, I must tell Queen Esther to warn the king." The two officers were arrested and hung.

Sometime later the king elevated the evil Haman to a high position and commanded that everyone was supposed to bow low when Haman walked by. However, Mordecai refused to bow down because a Jew only bows down to God. Haman got angry and stomped about. And he kept on stomping, until finally he got an idea: "I know," he said. "I'll trick the king into issuing an edict to kill all of the Jews, including Mordecai."

When Mordecai found out the king had decided to kill all of the Jews, he tore his clothes and wept, moaned and wailed. After doing this for a while, he explained the situation to Esther. At first she was frightened, but finally she said "I've got to put a stop to this."

Interestingly enough, the king had a hard time sleeping one night. He was tossing and turning and suddenly woke up. He grabbed for the nearest book which happened to be a history of his reign. He read the story about Mordecai saving his life and wondered aloud, "Hmmm... I wonder if I ever honored him."

He called, "Haman." Haman ran into the room. King Xerxes asked, "What should be done for the man the king delights to honor?" Haman thought the king was talking about him so he made up an elaborate plan to honor himself. The king liked Haman's plan and exclaimed,

ESTHER:
FOR SUCH
A TIME
AS THIS

"Good! I want you to see that Mordecai is honored in this way." So Haman was forced to give Mordecai honor. Now he was really mad at Mordecai and planned to hang him.

Meanwhile Esther planned a banquet for the king and she also invited Haman. The king, Haman and Esther were all sitting around a table, eating and drinking. Suddenly, the king asked, "What is your petition, Esther?" Esther asked the king boldly, "Please save my people from death." The king raged, "Who is this evil man who dares to kill my queen and her people?" Haman cringed and tried to sneak away. Esther pointed to the fleeing Haman and declared, "It is Haman who plans this evil deed!" The king listened carefully to Esther. He had the guard arrest Haman and he had him hung on the very gallows that he had built for Mordecai. Esther and Mordecai jumped for joy and yelled, "The Jews have been saved!"

A CLOSE LOOK AT THE KEY PLAYERS

1. How do you think God worked through Xerxes' seemingly unfair dismissal of Queen Vashti, his first wife?

....

....

....

2. Read Esther 5:9-14. How would you describe Haman?

....

....

....

If you were king, would you want him as your close advisor? What was he really interested in?

....

....

....

3. How was Esther treated as the queen (see Esther 4:11,15,16)?

....

....

....

How could this have changed if the king was displeased with her request to save the Jews?

....

....

....

4. How do you think Esther felt when Moredecai insisted that she conceal her Jewish identity?

....

....

....

5. What did Mordecai mean in Esther 4:14 when he warned Esther "For if you remain silent at this time, relief and deliverance for the Jews will arise from another place, but you and your father's family will perish. And who knows but that you have come to royal position *for such a time as this*?" (Italics added for emphasis.)

....

....

ESTHER:
FOR SUCH
A TIME
AS THIS

How does Esther's reply to Mordecai in verse 16 point out the serious danger she would be in?

....

....

....

So What?

1. How is God calling you to act "for such a time as this" to tell others about Him this week in...

....

....

....

Your home?

....

....

....

Your friendships?

....

....

....

Your school?

....

....

....

2. What might you lose if you tell others about Him?

....

....

....

3. Knowing what you might lose, why should you speak up?

....

....

....

T HINGS TO THINK ABOUT

1. What prevents us from obeying God when He calls us to do certain things at specific times?

....

....

....

2. What might be some of the consequences for others if we refuse to obey God?

....

....

....

3. What might be some of the consequences in our own lives if we refuse to obey God's call?

....

....

....

ESTHER:
FOR SUCH
A TIME
AS THIS

PARENT PAGE

LOOKING BACKWARD AND LOOKING FORWARD

The life of Esther demonstrates God's power to use us in our current circumstances to tell others about Him. Esther was able to use her position as queen to ask the king to save the Jewish people. Her cousin Mordecai challenged her in Esther 4:14 that she had come to her royal position "for such a time as this." Yet in bringing her request to the king, Esther made a difficult and brave choice (see Esther 4:16).

At times, being used by God means making a tough choice. That choice can have a tremendous influence on others.

Looking Backward

1. Looking back in your family's past, what choices have made a difference in your life together?

....

....

....

2. How would your life be different if you hadn't made those choices?

....

....

....

Looking Forward

1. What unique characteristics of your family might God want to use to help others know Him?

....

....

....

2. How can you cultivate an awareness of God's timing and the choices He wants you to make?

....

....

....

Session 10 "Esther: For Such a Time as This" Date...

JOB:
WHEN THE GOING GETS TOUGH

KEY VERSE

"'Though he slay me, yet will I hope in him.'" Job 13:15

BIBLICAL BASIS

Job 1:13-19; 2:7-9; 4:8; 8:6; 13:15; 20:3-5,27-29; 37:23,24; 38:8,9,25,26,36,37; 42:2,3,5; Hebrews 11:1,6

THE BIG IDEA

When the going gets tough, the tough run to the Lord!

AIMS OF THIS SESSION

During this session you will guide students to:
• Examine the necessity of trusting God;
• Discover how to focus on who God is, not why tough times happen;
• Implement trust in God in the toughest areas of their lives.

WARM UP

WHAT IS TOUGHER?—
Students think about the tough stuff of life.

TEAM EFFORT— JUNIOR HIGH/ MIDDLE SCHOOL

DEAR GOD,—
Students consider what they would say to God if they lost everything important to them.

TEAM EFFORT— HIGH SCHOOL

IMAGINE IF YOU LOST...—
An activity to help students understand how they would feel if they lost everything important to them.

IN THE WORD

TAKING ON THE TOUGH STUFF—
A Bible study that examines how to respond in tough times.

THINGS TO THINK ABOUT (OPTIONAL)

Questions to get students thinking and talking about why certain things happen to people.

PARENT PAGE

A tool to get the session into the home and allow parents and young people to discuss what they can learn from tough times in their families.

**JOB:
WHEN THE GOING
GETS TOUGH**

LEADER'S DEVOTIONAL

"Now faith is being sure of what we hope for and certain of what we do not see. And without faith it is impossible to please God, because anyone who comes to him must believe that he exists and that he rewards those who earnestly seek him" (Hebrews 11:1,6).

What are you doing right now that you could not do without the help of our supernatural God? When we think of the word "faith," we often think of the most incredible miracles we've ever heard about. I don't know about you, but I believe in those kinds of miracles of faith. Sometimes God chooses to heal a person who has cancer. In fact, I've even heard of God supernaturally giving a van extra gas mileage when a group of people were smuggling Bibles into a country where Bibles were forbidden. There are other times when people have just as much faith, but God chooses not to heal or do a miracle.

Faith is demonstrated by ordinary people doing extraordinary things through the power of God in their lives. Faith is Bob Wieland walking across America on his hands because he has no feet! Faith is Rachel deciding not to abort her baby even though her boyfriend pressed her to abort. Faith is Cheryl and Hank almost going all the way but deciding to remain virgins, even when they would really like to have sexual intercourse. Faith is Ted choosing not to cheat on exams anymore.

Faith is ordinary people being obedient even when it is hard. It's deciding not to drink or not to have sex before marriage even when "everyone else" is doing it. It's walking away from riches because God is calling you to be a missionary. Faith is asking God to help you overcome an eating disorder or to love the unlovable. Faith is placing all that you are, all that you can be and all that you do into the hands of God.

Faith is doing something or being someone that you could not do or be without the help of our supernatural God.

What are you doing in faith right now? Take a moment and ask God to make you an ordinary person doing extraordinary things for Him.

**"One person plus God is always a majority."
—Howard Hendricks**

JOB:
WHEN THE GOING GETS TOUGH

K EY VERSE
"Though he slay me, yet will I hope in him." Job 13:15

B IBLICAL BASIS
Job 1:13-19; 2:7-9; 4:8; 8:6; 13:15; 20:3-5,27-29; 37:23,24; 38:8,9,25,26,36,37; 42:2,3,5; Hebrews 11:1,6

T HE BIG IDEA
When the going gets tough, the tough run to the Lord!

W ARM UP (5-10 MINUTES)

What Is Tougher?
• Have students stand up. Tell them to respond to the question "What is tougher?" by moving to the side of the room that you indicate for their choices.
• As you read each pair of choices, indicate the left side of the room for those in the left column and the right side for those in the right column.
• Give a few seconds for them to make their decisions, then ask a few of them to explain their decisions.

Outdoor yard work	or	Indoor housework
A broken arm	or	A broken leg
An awful haircut	or	Awful acne
Losing $50	or	Losing your school I.D. card
Changing to a new school	or	Changing to a new church
Failing a class	or	Getting cut from a sports team

------- Fold -------

1. What is the difference between hearing about God and seeing God?

2. How had Job seen God?

So WHAT?
It Is Well with My Soul
Several decades ago, Horatio G. Spafford said good-bye to his wife and daughters as they boarded a ship crossing the Atlantic Ocean. To the dismay of Horatio and hundreds of others, the ship went down. There were few survivors. Horatio's wife was one of those few survivors. She sent her husband the following telegraph: "Ship went down. Both daughters lost. It is well."

Motivated by his wife's courage, Horatio wrote the following powerful and poignant text. His words have become the backbone of one of the most frequently sung hymns today.

> When peace like a river attendeth my way,
> When sorrows like sea billows roll;
> Whatever my lot, Thou hast taught me to say,
> "It is well, it is well with my soul."

1. What area in your life is tough for you right now?

2. What can you do about it?

Take two minutes to pray about that area. Begin your prayer to God by praying, "Even in this tough area of my life, it is well with my soul because..." Open your heart to anything God might want to let you know.

T HINGS TO THINK ABOUT (OPTIONAL)
• Use the questions on page 125 after or as a part of "In the Word."
If one of your non-Christian friends asked you the following questions, how would you respond?
1. Why do bad things happen to good people?

2. Why do good things happen to bad people?

3. Is God fair? Explain your answer.

P ARENT PAGE
• Distribute page to parents.

119

TEAM EFFORT—JUNIOR HIGH/MIDDLE SCHOOL (15-20 MINUTES)

DEAR GOD,

- Give each student a copy of "Dear God," on page 121 and a pen or pencil.
- Give them about seven to ten minutes to write their letters.
- After your students have written their letters, have them get into pairs and share what they've written.

Imagine you have just lost everything—your family, your friends, your possessions—and you have an extremely painful skin rash. You have the chance to write a letter to God letting Him know how you feel and asking Him any questions you want.

Dear God,

I feel...

My questions are...

....

Love,

TEAM EFFORT—HIGH SCHOOL (15-20 MINUTES)

IMAGINE IF YOU LOST...

- Distribute a piece of paper and a pen or pencil to each student.
- Give them two minutes to make a list of all the things in their lives that they are grateful for.

You may want to give them some examples, such as great friends or a new job.

- After two minutes, explain that they must cross off the following items from their own lists:

Friends	Musical abilities
Family	Sports abilities
Boyfriend/girlfriend	House
Good grades	Food
Job	Money
Car, bike, skateboard	Church youth group
Driver's license	Physical health
Clothes	Mental health

- Ask them to read aloud any other things they are grateful for. Have them cross off those items also. Discuss the following:

What are you left with?

Having just lost everything, what would you want to say to God?

....

IN THE WORD (25-30 MINUTES)

TAKING ON THE TOUGH STUFF

- Divide students into groups of three or four.
- Give each student a copy of "Taking on the Tough Stuff" on pages 122-124 and a pen or pencil, or display a copy using an overhead projector.
- Have students complete the Bible study in the small groups except for the "So What?" section which they will do individually.

Fold

WHAT WAS TOUGH FOR JOB?

The book of Job is one of the most well-known examples of what to do when the going gets tough.

1. Look up each verse and describe the tough circumstances Job faced.

Job 1:13-15

....

Job 1:16

....

Job 1:17

....

Job 1:18,19

....

Job 2:7,8

....

2. At what point do you think Job felt like screaming, "Enough is enough!?"

....

WHEN THE GOING GETS TOUGH, OTHERS MAY SAY...

Job was surrounded by people who meant well, but nonetheless gave some bad advice. Summarize the advice of each friend and evaluate its effectiveness.

Job's wife—Job 2:9

....

Eliphaz—Job 4:8

....

Bildad—Job 8:6

....

Zophar—Job 20:3-5,27-29

....

Elihu—Job 37:23,24

....

WHEN THE GOING GETS TOUGH, THE TOUGH RUN TO GOD

Faced with his overwhelmingly tough circumstances, Job asked God a logical question: "Why?" In fact, he asked Why 16 times.

In the book of Job, we read a similar word—who—59 times. Each time "who" is in reference to God. Job did not need to know precisely why these things happened to him. Instead, he relied on who God is (see Job 38:8,9,25,26,36,37 for examples).

After these statements, Job replies,

"I know that you can do all things; no plan of yours can be thwarted....Surely I spoke of things I did not understand, things too wonderful for me to know. My ears had heard of you but now my eyes have seen you" (Job 42:2,3,5).

T EAM EFFORT

DEAR GOD,

Imagine you have just lost everything—your family, your friends, your possessions—and you have an extremely painful skin rash. You have the chance to write a letter to God, letting Him know how you feel and asking Him any questions you want.

Dear God,

I feel...

_____

_____

_____

_____

_____

_____

_____

_____

My questions are...

_____

_____

_____

_____

_____

_____

_____

_____

_____

Love,

**JOB:
WHEN THE GOING
GETS TOUGH**

IN THE WORD

TAKING ON THE TOUGH STUFF

What Was Tough for Job?

The book of Job is one of the most well-known examples of what to do when the going gets tough.

1. Look up each verse and describe the tough circumstances Job faced.

Job 1:13-15

Job 1:16

Job 1:17

Job 1:18,19

Job 2:7,8

2. At what point do you think Job felt like screaming, "Enough is enough!"?

....

....

....

When the Going Gets Tough, Others May Say...

Job was surrounded by people who meant well, but nonetheless gave some bad advice. Summarize the advice of each friend and evaluate its effectiveness.

Job's wife—Job 2:9

....

....

Eliphaz—Job 4:8

....

....

Bildad—Job 8:6

....

....

Zophar—Job 20:3-5,27-29

....

....

Elihu—Job 37:23,24

....

....

....

When the Going Gets Tough, the Tough Run to God

Faced with his overwhelmingly tough circumstances, Job asked God a logical question: "Why?" In fact, he asked Why 16 times.

In the book of Job, we read a similar word—who—59 times. Each time "who" is in reference

JOB: WHEN THE GOING GETS TOUGH

to God. Job did not need to know precisely why these things happened to him. Instead, he relied on who God is (see Job 38:8,9,25,26,36,37 for examples). [1]

After these statements, Job replies,

> "I know that you can do all things; no plan of yours can be thwarted....Surely I spoke of things I did not understand, things too wonderful for me to know. My ears had heard of you but now my eyes have seen you" (Job 42:2,3,5).

1. What is the difference between hearing about God and seeing God?

_____

_____

_____

2. How had Job seen God?

_____

_____

_____

So What?

It Is Well with My Soul

Several decades ago, Horatio G. Spafford said good-bye to his wife and daughters as they boarded a ship crossing the Atlantic Ocean. To the dismay of Horatio and hundreds of others, the ship went down. There were few survivors.

Horatio's wife was one of those few survivors. She sent her husband the following telegraph: "Ship went down. Both daughters lost. It is well."

Motivated by his wife's courage, Horatio wrote the following powerful and poignant text. His words have become the backbone of one of the most frequently sung hymns today.

> When peace like a river attendeth my way,
> When sorrows like sea billows roll;
> Whatever my lot, Thou hast taught me to say,
> "It is well, it is well with my soul."

1. What area in your life is tough for you right now?

_____

_____

_____

2. What can you do about it?

_____

_____

_____

_____

Take two minutes to pray about that area. Begin your prayer to God by praying, "Even in this tough area of my life, it is well with my soul because... " Open your heart to anything God might want to let you know.

1. Adapted from Henry Gariepy, *Portraits of Perseverance* (Wheaton, Ill.: Scripture Press Publications, Victor Books, 1989), pp. 205-206.

T HINGS TO THINK ABOUT

If one of your non-Christian friends asked you the following questions, how would you respond?

1. Why do bad things happen to good people?

....
....
....

2. Why do good things happen to bad people?

....
....
....

3. Is God fair? Explain your answer.

....
....
....

JOB:
WHEN THE GOING
GETS TOUGH

ORDINARY
PEOPLE WITH
EXTRAORDINARY
QUALITIES

PARENT PAGE

WHISPERS AND SHOUTS

In many ways, what happened to Job in the Old Testament resembles what happened to the author C.S. Lewis in this century. The book of Job and Job's incredible emotional and intellectual wrestling with God echo a quote by C.S. Lewis: "God whispers to us in our joy and shouts to us in our pain."

C.S. Lewis knew about pain. He was a well-known British professor, theologian and author who had a broad speaking and writing ministry. Upon meeting one of his admirers, Joy, he fell in love with her and married her. Tragically, soon after they were married, Joy died of cancer. Truly C.S. Lewis experienced deep pain and knew God's power to comfort and heal.

1. As a family, read Job 13:15. What do you think Job would want to say to C.S. Lewis?

2. What do you think C.S. Lewis would want to say to Job?

3. What was a tough time that brought your family together?

4. What did you learn from this tough time?

5. What tough things are going on in your family at this moment?

6. What attitude does God want you to have in every tough time?

Session 11 "Job: When the Going Gets Tough" Date

DANIEL:
STANDING UP AND STANDING OUT

KEY VERSE

"Daniel answered, 'O king, live forever! My God sent his angel, and he shut the mouths of the lions. They have not hurt me, because I was found innocent in his sight. Nor have I ever done any wrong before you, O king.'

"The king was overjoyed and gave orders to lift Daniel out of the den. And when Daniel was lifted from the den, no wound was found on him, because he had trusted in his God." Daniel 6:21-23

BIBLICAL BASIS

Isaiah 6:8,9;
Ezekiel 22:30;
Daniel 1:1-17; 6:1-27

THE BIG IDEA

When you stand up for the Lord, you will stand out from the crowd.

AIMS OF THIS SESSION

During this session you will guide students to:

• Examine the pressures that keep them from standing up for the Lord in purity, integrity and godliness;
• Discover the ways they can stand out from the crowd;
• Implement a way to make a stand for the Lord this month.

WARM UP

STANDING ALONE—
An activity that examines how difficult it is to be alone when standing for the truth.

TEAM EFFORT— JUNIOR HIGH/ MIDDLE SCHOOL

THE BIG THREE—
A comparison of the influence of friends, parents and students' own thoughts.

TEAM EFFORT— HIGH SCHOOL

WHAT WOULD YOU STAND FOR?—
A probing examination of the freedoms that are most important to students.

IN THE WORD

STANDING UP AND STANDING OUT—
A Bible study about Daniel and the way he stood for the Lord in purity, integrity and godliness.

THINGS TO THINK ABOUT (OPTIONAL)

Questions to get students thinking and talking about the meaning and significance of God's protection and provision.

PARENT PAGE

A tool to get the session into the home and allow parents and young people to interview each other to learn about current pressures that discourage them from standing for the Lord.

DANIEL:
STANDING UP AND
STANDING OUT

LEADER'S DEVOTIONAL

"I looked for a man [or woman] among them who would build up the wall and stand before me in the gap on behalf of the land so I would not have to destroy it, but I found none" (Ezekiel 22:30).

Imagine for a moment being in Ezekiel's shoes, or I mean sandals! You hear the voice of the living God say that He is looking for someone to step forward and stand in the gap in order to build up the crumbled wall. God couldn't find anyone who had the courage to take on the task.

What would you do if God spoke to you and said He was looking for a man or a woman who could stand in the gap on behalf of today's youth? Are you willing to be in the minority of adults who will work with students for the living God? Our society is crumbling around us and the enemy is well-armed and well-funded, but on your side is the living Lord who cares deeply about the society in which His children are now residing. God needs to borrow a voice, a loving and caring arm, or perhaps some hands and feet to help reach this generation of young people. Why He would use someone like you and me is a complete mystery to me, but He still chooses to build His kingdom with us less-than-perfect types. In fact He tells us in His Word that He will supply the life-changing power and all you have to do is stand in the gap.

So let's review: Just like the days of Ezekiel, the world around us is crumbling and God is looking for ordinary people to do a most extraordinary task of standing in the gap for Him. He'll do the supernatural work, but He still needs a willing body. He offers you and me the same call He issued to Isaiah. Remember when Isaiah said, "Then I heard the voice of the Lord saying, 'Whom shall I send? And who will go for us?'" Do you remember Isaiah's response? It's the same response God is looking for today. "'Here am I. Send me!'" And God responded with "'Go and tell this people'"(Isaiah 6:8,9).

When we think of people like Isaiah and Ezekiel, we probably imagine larger-than-life personalities—the superstars of their day. I'm beginning to think that they were even more ordinary in looks and brains than the rest of the people. However, what made them stand out was an uncompromising commitment to take a stand for God. So what about you?

**"I am willing to go anywhere and do anything for Jesus Christ."
—Dave Hess, 17-year-old summer missionary**

DANIEL: STANDING UP AND STANDING OUT

KEY VERSE

"Daniel answered, 'O king, live forever! My God sent his angel, and he shut the mouths of the lions. They have not hurt me, because I was found innocent in his sight. Nor have I ever done any wrong before you, O king.'

"The king was overjoyed and gave orders to lift Daniel out of the den. And when Daniel was lifted from the den, no wound was found on him, because he had trusted in his God." Daniel 6:21-23

BIBLICAL BASIS

Isaiah 6:8,9; Ezekiel 22:30; Daniel 1:1-17; 6:1-27

THE BIG IDEA

When you stand up for the Lord, you will stand out from the crowd.

WARM UP (5-10 MINUTES)

STANDING ALONE

• The object of this exercise is to demonstrate how difficult it is to stand for your convictions when you feel alone.

• Draw the following diagram on the board, flipchart or overhead transparency:

Which Line Is Longer?

_____ Line A

_____ Line B

• Ahead of time, privately show four students the overhead diagram.

• Point out that Line A is clearly longer than Line B. However, explain that later on in class, when you ask them which line is longer, they should say the incorrect answer, "Line B."

--- Fold ---

	Standing up for the Lord Daniel 1:1-14	Standing out Daniel 1:15-17
In Purity		
In Integrity	Daniel 6:1,2,4,5	Daniel 6:3,4
In Godliness	Daniel 6:7-11	Daniel 6:21-23

1. Why was King Darius so distraught in Daniel 6:11-20?

2. How do you think Daniel felt after being thrown into the lions' den as it became dark and the lions began to growl in hunger?

3. How did Daniel's commitment to standing for the Lord benefit the kingdom in Daniel 6:26,27?

SO WHAT?

Take a few minutes to fill out your own personal table, describing how you can stand up for the Lord in purity, integrity and godliness.

I can stand for the Lord this month by...

In Purity:

In Integrity:

In Godliness:

1. How will taking these stands cause you to stand out from the crowd?

2. What negative consequences might you face for your decisions?

3. Given this, are you still ready to begin to take a stand this week?

Spend the remaining moments asking for God's strength and guidance to help you stand up for Him.

THINGS TO THINK ABOUT (OPTIONAL)

• Use the questions on page 134 after or as a part of "In the Word."

1. Do you believe that Daniel thought God would protect him in the lions' den? Why or why not?

2. Does God guarantee us protection when we take risky stands for Him? How do you know?

3. If taking a stand for God is no guarantee of protection, why should we stand up for Him at all?

PARENT PAGE

• Distribute page to parents.

• At the beginning of the session, explain that you need help from five students. Make sure that you choose the original four who have already seen the diagram, as well as one student who hasn't.

• Display the diagram on the overhead projector. Ask the five students to answer the question "Which line is longer?" Make sure you call on the original four students first. They should unanimously answer that Line B is longer. When you ask Student Number Five which line is longer, you may get the correct answer, Line A, or that person may give in to the peer pressure and answer the incorrect but popular answer, Line B.

• Have all five students be seated. Explain that you had prearranged the answers of the first four students.

1. Ask Student Number Five: What were you thinking as you heard the answers of the other four students?

....

2. Why did you answer as you did?

....

Explain that this same exercise has been done with hundreds of other students and adults and that most give in to peer pressure and give the obviously incorrect answer.

3. How does the pressure of the group influence our decisions?

....

⊤EAM EFFORT—JUNIOR HIGH/MIDDLE SCHOOL (15-20 MINUTES)

THE BIG THREE

• Give each student a copy of "The Big Three" on page 131 and a pen or pencil.

• Have students complete the page by themselves.

• After about five minutes, have students share their responses to the last item.

• Discuss the question.

Which of these big three influences would you listen to in the following areas:

	Friends	Parents	Myself
1. What to wear to school	___	___	___
2. What movie to see Saturday	___	___	___
3. What radio station to listen to	___	___	___
4. How to get the attention of the girl/guy you like	___	___	___
5. What to believe about God	___	___	___
6. What to do about a fight with a friend	___	___	___
7. Overall, who would you listen to the most?	___	___	___

How can God speak to you through your friends, your parents or your own thoughts?

....

⊤EAM EFFORT—HIGH SCHOOL (15-20 MINUTES)

WHAT WOULD YOU STAND FOR?

• Explain that this exercise is designed to help students answer the question "What would you stand for?"

• Write the following list of freedoms on the board, flipchart or overhead.

• Explain that they can only choose four that are so important that they would argue for that freedom, even if all of their friends opposed them.

• After the students have chosen their important freedoms, discuss the questions that follow.

    The freedom to eat whatever you want
    The freedom to drive
    The freedom to choose your own friends
    The freedom to go to church
    The freedom to keep your room as you want it
    The freedom to listen to whatever music you want
    The freedom to begin a student-led Bible club on your campus
    The freedom to pray

1. Picture yourself in a class debate in which you are the only one who stands for your four chosen freedoms. How would you feel?

....

2. What would prevent you from simply giving in to the majority opinion?

....

⌐N THE WORD (25-30 MINUTES)

STANDING UP AND STANDING OUT

• Divide students into groups of three or four.

• Give each student a copy of "Standing Up and Standing Out" on pages 132-133 and a pen or pencil.

• Have students complete the first part of the study with their groups.

• Allow five to ten minutes at the end for students to complete the "So What?" section by themselves.

As a young man, Daniel was ripped away from his home in Jerusalem and taken in captivity to Babylon. In this new and hostile land, Daniel repeatedly chose to stand up for his convictions, even when no one else stood with him. By taking such bold stands, he quickly stood out from the rest.

In this table, you see that Daniel stood out in three ways:

1. In **Purity**, by avoiding harmful influences;
2. In **Integrity**, by doing the right thing; and
3. In **Godliness**, by following God no matter what.

Fill out this table explaining how Daniel stood up for the Lord as well as how he stood out from the rest. Use these Scripture verses from the book of Daniel to be as specific as possible.

ORDINARY PEOPLE WITH EXTRAORDINARY QUALITIES

DANIEL: STANDING UP AND STANDING OUT

TEAM EFFORT

THE BIG THREE

Which of these big three influences would you listen to in the following areas:

	Friends	Parents	Myself
1. What to wear to school	___	___	___
2. What movie to see Saturday	___	___	___
3. What radio station to listen to	___	___	___
4. How to get the attention of the girl/guy you like	___	___	___
5. What to believe about God	___	___	___
6. What to do about a fight with a friend	___	___	___
7. Overall, who would you listen to the most?	___	___	___

How can God speak to you through your friends, your parents or your own thoughts?

....

....

....

**DANIEL:
STANDING UP AND
STANDING OUT**

IN THE WORD

STANDING UP AND STANDING OUT

As a young man, Daniel was ripped away from his home in Jerusalem and taken in captivity to Babylon. In this new and hostile land, Daniel repeatedly chose to stand up for his convictions, even when no one else stood with him. By taking such bold stands, he quickly stood out from the rest.

In this table, you see that Daniel stood out in three ways:

1. In Purity, by avoiding harmful influences,
2. In Integrity, by doing the right thing, and
3. In Godliness, by following God no matter what.

Fill out this table explaining how Daniel stood up for the Lord as well as how he stood out from the rest. Use these Scripture verses from the book of Daniel to be as specific as possible.

	Standing Up for the Lord	Standing Out
1. In Purity	Daniel 1:1-14	Daniel 1:15-17
2. In Integrity	Daniel 6:1,2,4,5	Daniel 6:3,4
3. In Godliness	Daniel 6:7-11	Daniel 6:21-23

1. Why was King Darius so distraught in Daniel 6:11-20?

2. How do you think Daniel felt after being thrown into the lions' den as it became dark and the lions began to growl in hunger?

3. How did Daniel's commitment to standing for the Lord benefit the kingdom in Daniel 6:26-27?

....

....

SO WHAT?

Take a few minutes to fill out your own personal table, describing how you can stand up for the Lord in purity, integrity and godliness.

I can stand for the Lord this month by...

In Purity:

....

....

In Integrity:

....

....

In Godliness:

....

....

1. How will taking these stands cause you to stand out?

....

....

2. What negative consequences might you face for your decisions?

....

....

3. Given this, are you still ready to begin to take a stand this week?

....

....

Spend your remaining moments asking for God's strength and guidance to help you stand up for Him.

THINGS TO THINK ABOUT

1. Do you believe that Daniel thought that God would protect him in the lions' den? Why or why not?

....

....

....

2. Does God guarantee us protection when we take risky stands for Him? How do you know?

....

....

....

3. If taking a stand for God is no guarantee of protection, why should we stand up for Him at all?

....

....

....

DANIEL:
STANDING UP AND
STANDING OUT

PARENT PAGE

STANDING STRONG

In the story of Daniel, we see a young man who refused to bow to pressure and instead took bold stands for the Lord. As a result, he stood out from the rest.

Read Daniel 6:1-23. What about Daniel helped him stand strong in the midst of a ton of peer pressure?

....

....

Peer pressure is not just a thing of the past; it is definitely a thing of the present. Ask each other these questions, making sure to be honest in your answers.

Student's questions for the parents:

1. What specific pressures did you face when you were a teenager?

....

....

2. What peer pressure do you face now, either at home, at work or in the neighborhood?

....

....

3. Do you think today's peer pressure is stronger, weaker or the same as when you were my age?

....

....

Parents' questions for the students:

1. Why do you think teenagers are more likely to listen to their friends or the media, than their parents or church?

....

....

2. What helps you stand up for the right thing?

....

....

3. In what area of your life do you wish you could get more advice or help from me as your parent?

....

....

....

....

....

Session 12 "Daniel: Standing Up and Standing Out"
Date ....

www.youthbuilders.com

Reach & Impact Young People, Strengthen Families and Youth Workers, and Change Lives Forever!

Training

YouthBuilders offers a full range of training events from one-day seminars to weeklong conferences designed to equip youth workers, parents, and students. For a complete listing of events, contact training@youthbuilders.com or visit www.youthbuilders.com.

YouthBuilders.com

A family-based youth ministry web destination where youth workers and parents can learn the latest in training methods for guiding and influencing today's youth; sign up for our FREE monthly Fresh Ideas Youth Worker newsletters and our Good Advice Parent newsletters that are full of practical information, encouragement and valuable insights; and check out the huge selection of proven resources. Youth workers and parents can easily print out the latest guidelines for helping young people navigate the challenges faced when growing up in today's world.

Resources

YouthBuilders has an incredible selection of helpful resources for youth workers, parents and students including training videos, devotionals, curriculum and books. Visit our web site for a complete description.

YouthBuilders Radio

Jim Burns' drama/commentaries are on stations across the United States and Canada. Through drama, music, commentaries, and humor, Jim's radio program provides guidance and counsel on the most current issues facing today's family. To find a local station visit www.youthbuilders.com.

www.youthbuilders.com • 1-800-397-9725

32236 Paseo Adelanto, Suite D, San Juan Capistrano, California 92675

More from Jim Burns, the Youth Ministry Expert!

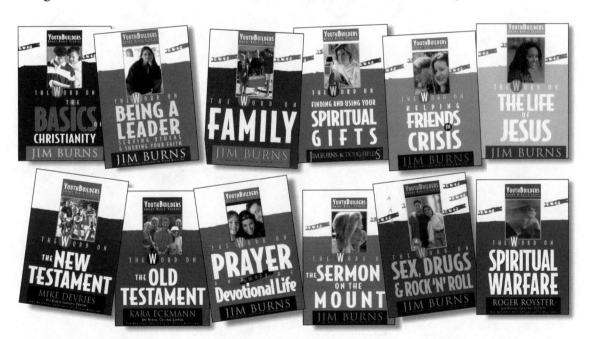

Wake 'Em Up!

This fresh-roasted blend of sizzling hot resources helps you turn youth meetings into dynamic events that kids look forward to. Successfully field-tested in youth groups and edited by youth expert **Jim Burns, Fresh Ideas** will wake 'em up and get your group talking.

Bible Study Outlines and Messages
ISBN 08307.18850

Case Studies, Talk Sheets and Starters
ISBN 08307.18842

Games, Crowdbreakers & Community Builders
ISBN 08307.18818

Illustrations, Stories and Quotes to Hang Your Message On
ISBN 08307.18834

Incredible Retreats
ISBN 08307.24036

Missions and Service Projects
ISBN 08307.18796

Skits and Dramas
ISBN 08307.18826

Worship Experiences
ISBN 08307.24044

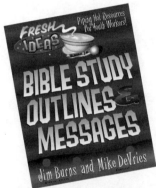

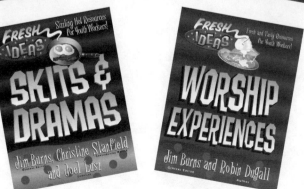

Gospel Light

To wake up your youth, contact your local Christian bookstore. **www.gospellight.com**

More Great Ways to Reach and Teach Young People

So You Want to Be a Wise Guy
An outrageous group study for junior high
Manual
ISBN 08307.29178

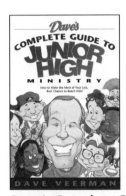

Dave's Complete Guide to Junior High Ministry
An all-in-one, practical, hands-on guide for everything relating to junior high ministry
Dave Veerman
Paperback
ISBN 08307.27604

GP4U (God's Plan for You)
A middle school/junior high group study
Kara Eckmann Powell
Reproducible
ISBN 08307.24060

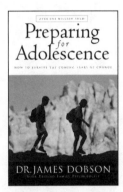

Preparing for Adolescence
Dr. James Dobson
Paperback
ISBN 08307.24974

Guide to Childhood Development
Mass
ISBN 08307.24990

Family Guide and Workbook
Manual
ISBN 08307.25016

Growth Guide Manual
ISBN 08307.25024

Group Guide
ISBN 08307.25008

Family Tape Pack—8 Audiocassettes
ISBN 08307.26357

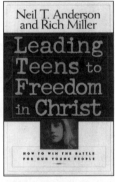

Leading Teens to Freedom in Christ
How to win the battle for our young people
Neil T. Anderson
and *Rich Miller*
Paperback
ISBN 08307.18400

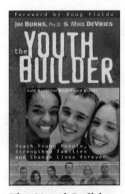

The YouthBuilder
Reaching young people for Christ and changing lives forever
Jim Burns
and *Mike DeVries*
Paperback
ISBN 08307.29232

Gospel Light

Available at your local Christian bookstore
www.gospellight.com

043021